D1547812

AUTOMATING SMALL LIBRARIES

JAMES SWAN

HIGHSMITH PRESS HANDBOOK SERIES

HP Highsmith® PRESS

Fort Atkinson, Wisconsin

Published by Highsmith Press LLC
W5527 Highway 106
P.O. Box 800
Fort Atkinson, Wisconsin 53538-0800
1-800-558-2110

© James Swan, 1996.
Cover by Mary Ann Highsmith.

2/97

The paper used in this publication meets the minimum requirements of
American National Standard for Information Science —
Permanence of Paper for Printed Library Material. ANSI/NISO Z39.48-1984.

Library of Congress Cataloging-in-Publication Data
Swan, James.
    Automating small libraries / James Swan.
      p. cm. – (Highsmith Press handbook series)
    Includes bibliographical references and index.
    ISBN 0-917846-78-8 (pbk. : alk. paper)
    1. Small libraries–United States–Data processing. 2. Small libraries–
United States–Automation. I. Title. II. Series.
  Z678. 93. S6S9 1996
  025' .00285–dc20 $15.00   96-31418
                                     CIP

ISBN 0-917846-78-8

Contents

Preface

What a blessing it would have been to have had a practical handbook on automating the small library before I started gathering information to automate the Great Bend Public Library! It could have saved us lots of work and kept us from exploring several options that turned out to be dead ends. We also might have decided to do some things differently.

We quickly learned that automating a library is not as easy as buying a few computers, connecting them together and then checking out books. You also have to put the library's bibliographic records, usually still found in the card catalog, on the computer, before you can use it to check out books and other materials.

We also learned that if you *really* want to automate your library, you can do it! In *Automating Small Libraries*, I've taken the experience I gained in Great Bend along with that gathered in working with other small libraries in the Central Kansas Library System. (My job also includes directing the Central Kansas Library System.) Each of the 50 member libraries have their own boards and budgets. Only three of the libraries have budgets over $400,000. The average budget for the rest of the libraries is just over $15,000. The librarians in five of the next largest libraries would like to automate now. They have had computers for a few years, but they need a plan to be able to put their books on the computer for the Online Public Access Catalog (OPAC) and to check out books with the computer system. The idea for this book came from the plan I developed to help them automate their libraries.

Drawing from the real experiences and pitfalls of automation, this book has been written to help you work your way through the process successfully. In the end, your patrons will be able to search for the information they want on the computer; put holds on materials, develop bibliographies for research, and find out what books they have checked out.

But before you can do all of these things, lots of information gathering, planning, decision-making and hard work has to happen. In the end, the effort is worth every minute you spend.

Automating the Great Bend Public Library

When I came to Kansas in 1977 to direct the Great Bend Public Library, I wanted to automate, but the price tag was around $500,000. In a few years it came down to about $200,000, but automation was still out of our price range. Even $100,000 seemed impossible. In 1994 the city turned over $80,000 they had been accumulating for the library. This was the window of opportunity we needed. In October 1994 the library board approved a plan to automate the library. The cost of the project was a little over $80,000.

It took over six months for us to gather the information and develop the plan. The first thing I did was to get permission from the board to look at automating the library. The second was to develop an introduction to automation to help the board understand what automation meant and what it could do for our library.

How to use *Automating Small Libraries*

Think of this book as a workshop. As you read, imagine that your board has sent you away to a two-day workshop to learn how to automate your library. The workshop is filled with checklists, suggestions and ideas that have worked for other librarians who have already automated. Impressions will come to you as you read; jot these ideas down. When you finish, you'll return to your library with enthusiasm and ideas you can try right away.

Don't forget to share the book with your staff and board members or principal. Then you can work together to develop a plan to involve others, and get the automation project moving.

Librarians everywhere are involved in exciting, successful automation projects. You can be, too. All you need is a push in the right direction. I hope this book gives you that push.

Overview

The purpose of this overview is to let you know where the book is headed. *Automating Small Libraries* is filled with recommendations, suggestions and options. It is your job to consider the suggestions and decide which options will work best for your library. The introduction and chapter 1 set the stage for your automation project by looking at library size and readiness, project costs and benefits as well as giving you a step-by-step project chart. In chapters 2 through 5 you will learn about your options in hardware, software and data conversion. The rest of the book will help you develop your plan and implement your automation project. With that introduction, I'd like to give you a closer look at the overall conversion process as we will be dealing with it in *Automating Small Libraries*.

Assessment: Inventory and weeding the collection   "Weeding and inventory are crucial precursors to retrospective conversion. Each bibliographic record costs money to create, process, update, and store. To create records for missing or outdated items is a waste of labor and funds."[1] In chapter 2 I will outline basic guidelines for the weeding and inventory of your collection with conversion in mind.

Selecting an automation system   A major question in selecting a library auto-mation system is How well will it meet your needs in the future? Results take time to measure. A system that meets your needs today may not work so well ten years from now. If the company fails to support the system you select after five years, what will it take to switch to a different system? Will your bar codes still work? Will you be able to move your bibliographic records to a new sys-tem? These are just a few of the questions you need to ask yourself before making a commitment to a company to use their software in your library.

Selecting the hardware and network configuration   The hardware and net-work configuration outlined in chapter 4 is the smallest network I can hon-estly recommend to a librarian who is planning to automate a small library. It consists of three computers connected to each other in a network. The rest of the hardware includes a bar code reader, a tape backup unit, a printer, and a concentrator that make it possible for the three computers to share infor-mation over the network.

Doing the data conversion   While no one will deny that buying computers and linking them together in a network represents a major capital expense, data conversion will cost you more time and money than you expect. Rightly so. When you bring up your online catalog for the public, you will want it to be the best that it can be. Chapter 5 presents a variety of cost-effective ways to convert data for your library.

Requesting bids   You can use the Request for Bids (or Request for Proposal) to gather information that will help you decide between two options. You may not be sure whether to send your records out for data conversion or to do them in-house. You could request bids for both methods and use price as one of the factors to help you decide. You could also request bids on differ-ent types of bar code scanners or computers with various enhancements. Chapter 6 covers the basics for preparing a Request for Bids document.

Developing the final plan   It is not wise to make decisions about one aspect of the plan without having the whole plan in mind. You have to be able to see your project from the beginning to the end and predict how everything will work. Chapter 7 focuses on the big picture of automating a library.

Funding or fundraising   People in small libraries may have been forced to wait because they couldn't afford to automate. Indeed, "sticker shock" seems to be the biggest obstacle to moving ahead with automating any size library. If this is a problem for your library, we have some funding ideas in chapter 8.

Implementation   After your plan is approved, you have to order and install the various components of the automation project and begin data conver-sion. You may want to develop a timeline for implementation similar to the one we created for Great Bend (see appendix D). It will help you focus on the activities you need to accomplish and on the order in which they need to be done.

Enhancements   Once you get your system up and running, you are sure to think of many enhancements to make your system work better for you and your customers. As you find the money and as new products come along you will be able to add devices and reference tools that can enhance the quality of the service your library offers. Possible enhancements are discussed in chapter 10.

Evaluation   After the system has been up and running for about six months it is time to evaluate your progress. Ask yourself: What went well? What could we have done differently? What can we do now to make automation work better for our patrons and ourselves? Involve the staff, the board and the customers in the process. You will learn some things that will help you in the evaluation process in chapter 11.

This overview was designed to let you know what to expect in the rest of the book. Feel free to skip some chapters if you want and get into the information you think will benefit you the most. The most important thing to remember as you read is to look for the green lights and figure a way to make the idea work for you.

Notes

1. John M. Cohn, Ann L. Kelsey, and Keith Michael Fiels. *Planning for Automation: A How-To-Do-It Manual for Librarians*, New York: Neal-Schuman, 1992.

Introduction

The scope of *Automating Small Libraries*

Automating Small Libraries uses a step-by-step approach that breaks the process into phases for librarians and trustees who want to automate their library. If you are able to use the suggestions here, the whole process will be less daunting. You don't even need a computer to begin; you can get started by assessing your need and your readiness. I'd like to begin by first defining small libraries as I will be addressing them for the purposes of this book.

What is small?

While small libraries are the primary focus of this book, librarians in all sizes of libraries may benefit from using the ideas discussed here. If you *think* you work in a small library, you probably do. For the purposes of this book, we are defining small libraries as libraries serving communities of 25,000 or less.[1] Libraries of this size usually have budgets of less than $400,000. Many small libraries are much smaller than this, but their librarians can still benefit from the information about automation we will cover here.

From my experience with small libraries, I have learned that libraries in towns from about 1,000 people and up, with budgets of around $50,000 and up, might be able to benefit from and be able to afford an automation project like the one I will be describing.

What type of automation systems are used in small libraries?

Because small libraries cannot usually afford mainframe or mini-computers, the scope of *Automating Small Libraries* includes only those library automation systems that operate under DOS or Windows, using a network of personal computers (PCs). I have developed a plan that enables a librarian in a small library to complete an automation project for approximately $12,000 to $20,000. The actual cost will depend on the number of workstations and additional equipment, which automation software is selected, and the method used for data conversion.

JARGON: By necessity this book will contain some automation jargon and technical words. The words that appear to be jargon will be defined in a shaded sidebar in the margin the first time they are used, and included in a glossary at the back of the book. Other information will appear in unshaded sidebars.

DOS (or MS-DOS) is the disk operating system, a program used by the computer to control the access and transmission of data to and from the disk and the computer.

WINDOWS is an operating system developed by Microsoft; it allows the use of graphics which are more user-friendly than DOS.

(See glossary for more detailed descriptions.)

This is not a technical book. We will not look at the design of a computer or how data is stored. We are not concerned about word processing or the details of telecommunications or how the Internet works. If you are like me, you understand computers well enough to know that they are wonderful tools to help librarians give people what they want when they come to the library. If you are like me, you also probably need someone to help trouble-shoot computer problems. If that is true, find someone on the library staff or someone in your community who can help you find your way through the maze of technical gobbledygook. Find someone who can give you the tools you need to make automation work, and then learn as much as you can about making those tools fit the needs of your library and your community.

> **This book will help you find the real costs, but you can count on everything costing more than you think it will.**

What is the cost of automating?

If your library budget is between $50,000 and $600,000, and you know you cannot afford $100,000 or more for one of the larger systems that run on a mainframe or mini-computer, *Automating Small Libraries* can help you. Even if you can afford more than $100,000 for a larger system this book can help you to create an automation process that will work for your library.

Here is an approximate breakdown of the cost for a minimal system:

Minimum Automation System Costs	
Automation software	$3,500 to 10,000
Three computer workstations	5,000
Printer	600
Bar code reader	600
Concentrator and cabling	500
Tape backup unit and tapes	300
CD-ROM bibliographic utility	500
Bar code labels for 10,000 books	300
Contingency	700
Total	**$12,000 to 18,500**

Later we will discuss the reasons for automation costs in greater detail. Right now you need to know that you can automate for between $12,000 and $20,000 if you handle the data conversion in-house. It will cost more if you send your records out for data conversion (see chapter 5).

Steps to Automation

Completing an automation project is not as linear as you might think. You won't find yourself accomplishing one task or making a single decision before moving onto the next. While a variety of activities can be happening at the same time, it helps to proceed in a certain order. Most projects begin with where you are now and take steps that move the organization from the status quo toward a new desired position. We will begin with an assessment of the current collection that includes a careful weeding and inventory.

While you are working on this, it may be convenient to begin looking at software and hardware options. In that way, by the time you get to the point of developing the final plan, you will know which software and hardware you want to use. You might even continue your weeding project as you work to put your books on the computer.

To get an overview of the major parts of the conversion process, see the chart on the next page. We'll be covering each of these items in turn, but you may find it helpful to return to page 4 from time to time for an overall view.

Once you have decided to automate your library, you will begin a process that will take from one to two years. You will be moving through the steps shown in the list here and detailed in the rest of the book. But, before you ask someone to write the check, look at the questions and readiness issues discussed in chapter 1—then take the Automation Readiness Test to see if you are really ready to automate.

Notes

1. Bernard Vavrek, Director of the Information Futures Institute at Clarion University, (Clarion, Pennsylvania) uses this definition for small libraries in the work he does.

AUTOMATION STEPS	TARGET START	COMPLETED
Study Automation Choices		
Take the automation Readiness Test. (Chapter 1)		
Look at your actual and potential resources to determine if you can afford to automate. (Introduction, Chapter 1)		
Assess you current collection, weed and inventory. (Chapter 2)		
Decide what you want the automation system to do. (Chapter 3)		
Gather information from automation system vendors. (Chapter 3)		
Make Automation Selections and Create for Plan for Implementation		
Develop a Request for Bids (Request for Proposal). (Chapter 6)		
Evaluate and compare bids. (Chapter 6)		
Select a system that meets the needs of the library. (Chapter 3)		
Review hardware and networking options. (Chapter 4)		
Secure hardware information and pricing. (Chapter 4)		
Prepare the library's collection for data conversion. (Chapter 5)		
Develop a formal plan for board approval. (Chapter 7)		
Develop plan for funding automation project. (Chapter 8)		
Create a process for implementation. (Chapter 9)		
Decide on staff training. (Chapter 9)		
Implement Finalized Plans and Complete Installation and Training		
Accept bids and order components (Chapter 7)		
Secure services of computer network consultant. (Chapter 9)		
Design wiring for electrical power to computers. (Chapter 4)		
Design cabling to network components. (Chapter 4)		
Develop workflow and procedure for data conversion. (Chapter 9)		
Install computer network. (Chapter 4)		
Determine how to enter borrower information on the computer. (Chapter 9)		
Consider furniture needs. (Chapter 6)		
Develop new borrower registration forms. (Chapter 9)		
Set a realistic date for bringing up the system for the public. (Chapter 9, Appendix D)		
Prepare publicity and public relations. (Chapter 9 and 10)		
Evaluate Progress and Make Plans for Enhancements		
Maintain the system. (Chapter 9)		
Decide on enhancements to the system. (Chapter 10)		
Review and change policies prompted by the automation project. (Chapter 11)		
Develop a process for evaluating and refining the system. (Chapter 10)		

Figure 1: Automation Steps.

The Decision to Automate

Chapter 1

When is it desirable to automate?

I remember a time in 1963 when I was stranded in Dallas without a car for about a week. I had some appointments to keep, so I set out on foot in the middle of the day. As I walked along the sidewalk I notice that city buses came along about every fifteen minutes. I wasn't sure what the fare was or where the bus would take me. After about an hour of walking, I finally waited at a bus stop for the next bus and asked the driver if he was headed in the direction I wanted to go. His route went right by my destination. I could have gotten on any of the buses on that route several miles back. For the same fare of twenty cents, I could have ridden from my home to my appointment. My main problem was uncertainty about when to get on the bus.

That is sort of the way it has been with libraries and computers—we don't know whether it is better to buy now or wait until the next level of computers comes out. During the 1970s and early 1980s when library technology was still in its infancy, and by comparison very expensive, when to automate posed a real quandary for most librarians. Microcomputers were just coming on the market and had only limited computing capacity. There was a plethora of operating systems, and some of them weren't very adaptable for libraries.

Now, librarians in large libraries have been automating for years. The overwhelming task of maintaining their card catalogs and handling thousands of circulation cards every day forced them into automation. The technology was available and they could afford it. *Isn't it about time smaller libraries automated, too?* They have cumbersome card catalogs, and their mounting circulation is no less a burden to their librarians. Affordable technology is now available to any librarian who has the will to automate, even the smallest library. You don't have to reinvent the wheel. Automation systems are available today that are more than capable of handling the automation needs of small libraries.

Over the next several pages you will find questions, lists and a readiness test, all designed to help you focus on the automation needs of your library and community. This is followed by a list of benefits, some you may have already been aware of, and some others that will hopefully give you new ideas

Our first microcomputer was a TRS-80 Model III sold by Radio Shack. It was too small for library circulation or an online catalog, but we did manage to develop a "home grown" overdue notice system that we used for about ten years. We were happy because it was much better than typing individual letters to delinquent borrowers. When software glitches finally caused us to find another solution, we vowed that we would never go back to typing individual overdue notices.

to build on. You may want to compile a similar list of your own—and add the things that I have missed. And finally, you will find an Automation Readiness Test, which will help you to assess your readiness to begin an automation project in your library today.

How do you assess your current collection and level of service? Would it benefit from automation?

Is the population of your community and the use of your library growing, or have both leveled off?

If these are not increasing, perhaps you simply need to improve your manual system. Population considerations are important to any library automation plan, but don't let this single issue keep you from automating your library.

Are you adding staff on a regular basis in order to keep up with the paperwork?

An automated system will not eliminate any staff, but it may lower the rate at which you add more people. Even if your staff has remained constant because of budget constraints, they may be feeling the press of increased work.

Is your manual system functional and are your patron records in good shape?

Never commit to automation in the hope that it will straighten out your messes. Conversion to automation must happen from a clean and functional system. If it doesn't, you will end up with an automated mess! When we visited other libraries to look at their automation systems, we found this last statement is absolutely true. One library had automated to get out from under the heavy burden of a manual circulation system. They used smart bar codes, but they only had enough money to do the data conversion for part of their collection. They brought up the automated circulation module with only about half their books in the system. When patrons came to the circulation desk with a stack of books to check out, they had to wait while the circulation staff added books that were not in the computer to the system. The staff, in their haste to check out books, made lots of typographical errors. They had exacerbated their circulation problem, not solved it—at least until they could complete their data conversion and clean up their catalog.

Is your collection fairly new?

The newer the material, the easier it is to convert the records to an automated system. Machine-readable records are more readily available for newer materials.

Do you have the expertise to maintain the equipment locally?

Support is necessary! Someone on your staff needs to know more about computers than how to turn them on. More importantly, you need someone in town you can call on for help when the system goes down. This could be the person who installed the hardware, someone from the regional library system or the state library, or just a friend who knows enough about your system to troubleshoot problems. You will also want prompt reliable support from your software vendor. More on that later.

SMART BAR CODES are bar code labels that have been created from the library's bibliographic records. They usually have the title of the book and the call number printed on them. They are bar codes that have been linked to a specific bibliographic record in your library.

DUMB BAR CODES are bar code labels that do not have a bibliographic record linked to them when they are purchased. You can purchase them by the thousands or make them yourself as you need them.

DATA CONVERSION is the process of putting your bibliographic records, the contents of the card catalog, on the computer and linking those records to a bar code you put on the book. See chapter 5.

Are you really doing enough business in the library to make this expenditure worthwhile? Or would the money be better spent elsewhere—like additional staff or more materials.

Whenever you buy something for your library, you have to remember that it costs whatever you pay for it, plus whatever you could have bought with the money you just spent. The less money you have to spend, the more critical spending priorities become.

Do you know your real needs and your budget—not just for the purchase of the computers, but for conversion of records and maintenance?[1]

Data conversion will cost more time and money than you think. System maintenance will also cost more than small libraries are used to—especially if you have to hire a computer consultant who charges $50 or more per hour. Take a good look at your budget and make sure you have enough in the contingency to cover unexpected costs.

Benefits of Automation

Automation can mean more to the library and its patrons than computerizing the card catalog and checking out books. Here is a short list of the benefits that automation can provide to you and your libary's patrons.

- Increase access to information through improved indexing.
- Enhance research techniques through automated access to sophisticated tools, such as CD-ROM products and online databases.
- Offer circulation status to patrons using the online catalog.
- Enhance the quality of reference service by giving the staff quicker and more complete access to the entire collection.
- Offer dial-up access from homes, schools, or other libraries.
- Create accurate lists of materials patrons have checked out, quickly and easily.
- Place reserves on books automatically.
- Verify patron information automatically with every transaction.
- Maintain the privacy of patron information.
- Tell patrons when a book that is checked out is expected back.
- Check books in and out faster.
- Generate overdue notices automatically.
- Give patrons the option of searching the collection by format, e.g., video, audiotapes, software.
- Simplify borrower registration.
- Decrease the time required for conducting the inventory.
- Eliminate filing cards in the circulation files and card catalog.
- Maintain the public access catalog with less time and effort.
- Provide the opportunity for public access to the Internet.

The INTERNET is a telecommunication network linking thousands of local and regional computer networks around the world. The Internet is used by students, scholars, researchers and reference librarians to access information that is in electronic format. Computers in libraries can access millions of pieces of information, data files, and graphics through an Internet provider.

If you want the benefits of automation for your library you have to be totally committed to the project. You have to want to do it. You have to want to do it more than you want a new library or new carpet for the one you have. And you can. Take this Automation Readiness Test to see if you really need to automate.

Automation Readiness Test

1. __ Yes __ No Do your patrons come into your library and ask where the computerized card catalog is?

2. __ Yes __ No Do people have to stand in line to check out books?

3. __ Yes __ No Do you have to give an unsatisfactory answer when patrons ask what books they have checked out?

4. __ Yes __ No Do you have a cumbersome or non-existent "hold system?"

5. __ Yes __ No Are patrons disappointed when you can't tell them if a book is in the library or checked out?

6. __ Yes __ No Do you spend more time filing catalog cards and circulation cards than you do helping patrons?

7. __ Yes __ No Do you have more checkout cards to file than you can file during regular library hours?

8. __ Yes __ No Does your staff seem overworked and stressed out because of the work load?

9. __ Yes __ No Have you been thinking about automating your library for three years or more?

10. __ Yes __ No Do you think you can find $10 to $20 thousand for automation over the next three years?

Answer Code:

If 7 to 10 answers were yes:
You need to automate now. Don't worry about the money. Make the plans and the money will come.

If 4 to 6 answers were yes:
You probably need to automate. Maybe not right away, but if you want to and you can find the money, do it.

If 1 to 3 answers were yes:
You probably don't need to automate. You can probably manage with your manual catalog and circulation processes.

How do librarians who have automated feel about their decision?

I surveyed of over 50 librarians from small libraries who had automated, and none indicated that they were able to reduce staff because of automation. Most were very loyal to the selection they had made for automation software. All of them, without exception, encouraged their fellow librarians to automate their libraries. These librarians would never want to go back to the way things were before automation. The difference between being automated and not is like the difference between the sun and the moon.

If you took the Automation Readiness Test and scored above six, you probably want to automate now. Few advantages can be gained by waiting any longer. Hardware that is powerful enough for automating a small library is plentiful and affordable. Automation software for small libraries has matured, having been on the market for years. New releases and upgrades come out three or four times a year. It is reliable and affordable. So why wait?

Developing your plan

Developing an automation proposal for your library is a lot of work, and you can't delegate very much of it. You have to gather as much information as you can and work with it yourself until you understand it. Then you can develop a proposal the board will understand. This means talking with a lot of people who know what they are doing and letting them help you understand how library automation works. Some of them will have a vested interest in selling you something, yet they will spend the time to help you understand what you need to know to develop your plan.

You start by deciding what you want automation to do for your library. You should be able to succinctly state in one short paragraph what kind of business your library is in and how automation will help you accomplish your purposes.

Early in the process you need to meet with the staff and discuss what functions you want to automate. This valuable process provides a sounding board for your ideas as well as creating staff commitment to the project. This commitment is a necessary element further down the line when the data conversion process seems to take forever or enthusiasm seems to wane.

Don't forget to focus on the customer

All reasons for automation should focus on customers. Automated circulation gives patrons faster checkout, quicker status reports on books they have on loan, automatic holds on materials, etc. The online public access catalog makes research easier for them. The point here is to help patrons see automation as something that helps them, not just makes circulation easier for the staff.

Moving ahead

Automating a small library may seem risky, but it isn't. It has become just a matter of time. Sooner or later real libraries—libraries that give quality reference service and are more than just "reading rooms"—will be automated. Not necessarily because the librarian wants to checkout books using the computer, but because library automation is a powerful reference tool and library patrons deserve the best library service their community can afford. If you have the money, the backing of the board or administration and the staff, and most of all, you want to do it, then automate your library now! Get on the bus!

SOFTWARE RELEASE OR UPGRADE includes enhancements to the software made by the software company to make the software work better or perform new functions. It is sort of like buying a new edition of a reference book.

Tips on Getting Started

1. Gather as much information as you can from printed sources. Check the Jan/Feb 1996 issue of *Library Technology Reports* This issue reviews PC-based library automation systems. There are some additional sources to get you started at the end of this chapter.

2. Write the vendors and request product information, a list of their clients, and a sample disk of their program. Within days you will get more information than ever thought you wanted. They will send you booklets to help you sell your board on automation.

3. Visit other libraries that have installed the automation systems you are seriously considering. Call other librarians around the country to learn the strengths and weaknesses of the systems they are using. Automation software companies will furnish lists of their customers. Develop a list of questions and start calling. Find other libraries, not on client lists, that are using software you are considering. Call these librarians, too. After all, you don't want to hear just from the totally satisfied customers the vendors have selected.

Notes

1. In a talk Susan Wills gave at the Second Annual Western Kansas Library Technology Conference, she asked librarians seven questions about automation. I have used her questions and added my comments to frame the discussion of this section of the book.

Suggested reading

Conference on Integrated On-line Library Systems. Compiled by David C. Genaway, Medford, New Jersey, 1990.

Fouty, Kathleen, *Implementing an Automated Circulation System: A How-to-Do-It Manual.* New York: Neal-Schuman, 1994.

Freedman, Maurice J. ed. "Library Automation Five Case Studies," *Library Journal* Special Report #22. New York: R.R. Bowker.

Gervasi, Anne, and Betty Kay Seibt, *Handbook for Small Rural, and Emerging Public Libraries.* Phoenix: Oryx Press, 1988.

Guide to Library Automation: Step-by-Step Introduction, 2nd ed. Caledonia, Minnesota: Winnebago Software Company, 1995.

Hildreth, Charles R. *Library Automation in North America: A Reassessment of the Impact of New Technologies in Networking.* New York: Saur, 1987.

The Librarians Yellow Pages. Larchmont, New York: Garance, Inc. Annual.

Library Automation in the Five Smaller Arrowhead Library System Libraries: A Report Prepared for the Arrowhead Library System. Janesville, Wisconsin: R. Walton and Associates, 1985.

Little Book of Library Automation, Monterey, California: McGraw-Hill Systems, 1994.

Rice, James, *Introduction to Library Automation.* Littleton, Colorado: Libraries Unlimited, 1984.

Sager, Donald J. *Small Libraries: Organization and Operation,* 2nd ed. Fort Atkinson, Wisconsin: Highsmith Press, 1996.

White, Howard S. ed. *Library Technology Reports.* Chicago: ALA. (January -February 1996).

Inventory and Weeding

Chapter 2

Have your ever seen a vegetable garden that was so full of weeds that you could barely see the good plants? It made you want to walk away. I have been in libraries that were so full of books that nobody wanted that I want to walk out. Weeding your library collection is a little like weeding a garden. The garden is more attractive and produces better results when it is weeded often.

When I was a child, I learned that a weed is a plant that grows where it is not wanted. In a garden you remove the weeds so the best plants will grow. In a library, you remove unwanted or unattractive books so people will find the newer books. You want people to come into your library and find books they want and check them out. Your job is to decide which items to keep and which ones to throw away.

Why is weeding in a book about automation?

The only reason we even mention weeding at all is because it is senseless to create bibliographic records and put them on a computer if the books are worn out, damaged or otherwise unsuitable for use. You will also want to do an inventory to make sure that the books are still in the collection before you go to the trouble of putting them on the computer.

You will spend more staff time and library money on data conversion than any other single component of your automation project. That is why it is absolutely essential to do a thorough, maybe even heartless, job of weeding the collection. You will be glad you spent the time to take a good look at every book in the library. Your collection will be more attractive and more useful to your patrons without some of the books you now have.

Some libraries have books that have been discarded from other libraries. The spines are dingy. The pages are brown and nobody bothers to give them a second look. When a few new books are put on the shelf with these old books, the new books are lost to the patrons. If librarians severely weed their collections, their circulation will go up. Some have had the faith to try it and found that weeding really works.

You don't have to wait until you get approval to automate your library to

In *Planning for Automation*, John M. Cohn says, "Weeding and inventory are crucial precursors to retrospective conversion. Each bibliographic record costs money to create, process, update, and store. To create records for missing or outdated items is a waste of labor and funds." [1]

start weeding and doing your inventory. You can work on your inventory or weeding project while you are working on your automation plan. At the Great Bend Public Library, we spent about five years on weeding and inventory before we developed our plan to automate. When the opportunity came to automate, we were ready. You may not need five years, but if you start right now, you may be ready when the chance to automate comes to your library.

If you already know how to weed your library collection and how to conduct an inventory, you can skip the next few pages. On the other hand, you may find a few gems that will help you; such as the Flow Chart for Weeding located in appendix A.

Basic guidelines

Here are some basic weeding guidelines prepared for small public libraries for our system by Donald B. Reynolds.[2]

Remember this very important first step: The library board must be kept informed of this ongoing effort to strengthen the library's collection.

Some of the specific advice is to weed:

- Books of antiquated appearance which might discourage use.
- Badly bound volumes with soft, pulpy paper and/or shoddy binding.
- Badly printed books, including those with small print, dull or faded print, cramped margins, poor illustrations, or paper that is translucent so that the print shows through.
- Worn-out books whose pages are dirty, brittle, or yellow, with missing pages, frayed binding, broken backs, or dingy or dirty covers.

Weeding of superfluous or duplicate volumes:

- Unneeded duplicate titles.
- Inexpensive reprints.
- Highly specialized books when the library holds more extensive or more up-to-date volumes on the same subject.
- Superfluous books on subjects of little interest to the local community.

Weeding based on poor content:

- When information is dated.
- When information is unsuitable.
- When improved editions exist.

Weeding based on age alone:

- Almanacs and yearbooks that have been superseded.
- Travel books after ten years.
- Junior encyclopedias from three to five years.
- Senior encyclopedias at least every five years. Suspect and re-read any nonfiction title that is more than five years old, taking into account actual information changes and availability of up-to-date materials.

Discarding materials

When you remove an item from the collection you can't just throw it in the trash. Unless it is a duplicate, you need to remove the shelflist card and all cards associated with the item from the card catalog. Then you need to mark the item in such a way that it won't find its way back into your library, such as "**DISCARDED**" or "**REMOVED**." You may be able to offer it in a book sale or take it to a recycling location. Whatever you do with the books should be environmentally responsible.

Weeding based on appearance

The most universally accepted criterion for weeding is based on the appearance of a book. Often, however, this criterion calls for caution to avoid discarding rare and/or historically important books, and for judgment to determine whether or not the book should be replaced or rebound.

Weeding based on use patterns:

- Books not circulated in three years that do not appear in a standard book list.
- Books not necessary for reference or historical perspective.

Weeding suggestions for the main Dewey Classes

000s, General Reference Works: Discard encyclopedias and bibliographies that are ten years old or older. If you feel you have an exception, keep the books. Discard yearbooks and almanacs when you have newer editions.

100s-200s, Religion and Philosophy: Keep systems of philosophy, of theology, scriptures, popular self-help guides, and anything your customers use.

300s, Social Sciences: Keep basic materials on customs and folklore. Keep a close eye on education, economics, investment, taxation, etc. Update them when they become obsolete which could be a few years after publication. You may choose to keep historical works on economics, political science, education and transportation, if there is a need.

400s, Language: Keep unabridged dictionaries unless they are in poor physical condition. Discard abridged scholastic dictionaries after five years or more. Keep old grammar books only if they are first editions or have historical value.

500s, Pure Science: Get rid of books with outdated information or theories. Discard general works for which you have a newer comparable edition. Keep textbooks for up to five years. Books on botany and natural history retain their value with age so don't discard them without a second look.

600s, Applied Science: Most of the material in this section will be obsolete in five to ten years. Patrons have a critical need for up-to-date materials, especially on the topics of cancer and other serious or chronic diseases. Keep cookbooks if they are used. Watch the use patterns in the areas of home economics, gardening, and crafts.

700s, Arts, Music, Hobbies, etc.: Don't discard books in the fine arts unless their poor physical condition makes it necessary. Don't keep books that have been mutilated. If you do you will invite others to treat your books the same way.

800s, Literature: Keep literary history, unless you have better, newer titles on the same topics. Discard works of novelists, poets, and dramatists that are no longer read by your patrons.

900s, History: Keep histories that have become literary classics. Keep everything related to local history, local family history, or local genealogy.

Biography: Keep collected biographies. Keep only the best of what you have of individual biographies of people who may no longer be in the limelight. Keep anything that may be useful for local history.

This section is not meant to be an exhaustive treatise on weeding, but rather a short summary for librarians who are planning to automate their

KEEPING CRITERIA

If we know what to keep, we can weed the rest. While weeding the collection, keep the following in mind:

1. The fact that a book has not circulated during the past three years is not proof that is not needed, since potential circulation value may still exist.

2. Keep a title if it is listed in one of the standard catalogs. (e.g., *Public Library Catalog, Children's Catalog,* etc.)

3. Keep a title if it is of historical community interest, regardless of condition.

4. If a title is being used frequently (although meeting other criteria for being weeded), it should probably be retained.

5. Having something is not always better than having nothing. Use interlibrary loan.

libraries. If you feel you need more help, get of a copy of *The CREW Method* listed in the suggested readings at the end of this chapter.

Collections in small libraries are rarely considered the last resource for serious researchers. The final test should be in the mind of the librarian and his or her relationship with the library's patrons. Weeding guidelines are no more than suggestions. Don't spend money and time putting a book on the computer that no one will ever check out again.

Conducting the inventory

If there is anything worse than adding a bibliographic record to your database for a book that should have been discarded, it is adding a book that you don't even have in your library. If you plan to use smart bar codes an accurate inventory is absolutely necessary. I know of a librarian who was planning to automate. One of the first things she did was to send the library's shelflist off for data conversion. A good first step—provided the shelflist was accurate. The library had over 200,000 titles, but they had not conducted an inventory in over ten years. When the database came back, ready to load on the automation system, it contained thousands of records for which there were no books on the shelves. Along with the database came smart bar codes, and so the library ended up with thousands of orphaned bar code labels. They were able to bring their automation system up in a matter of weeks, but their database was filled with thousands of records for which there were no books on the shelf.

I believe if they had it to do over again, they would enlist the help of all staff members and complete an inventory before they sent their shelflist for conversion. It would have saved them thousands of dollars, and a lot of work cleaning up the database and trying to find books that aren't there.

Finding the time to inventory

Most of the librarians I surveyed commented on the necessity of having an up-to-date inventory before beginning an automation project. Look at it this way. This will be the last time you will spend this much time doing an inventory. After automating, you will be able to do an inventory in about one-tenth the time it now takes. You will simply scan the bar codes of the items in the stacks and load the scanned data on the computer. You will then generate a report that will give you a list of missing books. (See chapter 5 on the placement of the bar code label, and its importance for inventory.)

If you are in a "one-person" library and you are the one person, finding the time to do an inventory may be difficult. I would suggest that you close the library or come in when the library is closed to do the inventory. You may be able to recruit a volunteer to help you. The process seems to go much faster when two people work together on it.

Inventory time is a good time to add unique numeric identifiers if they are not already on the shelflist. If you use a CD-ROM utility, the numbers are essential. Either way, these numbers will be the quickest way to find a complete MARC record for your holdings. You should add them to the shelflist cards if they aren't there.

ORPHANED BAR CODES are smart bar code labels for which the library has no books. They are created when the books they would normally be attached to are lost or stolen from the collection without the loss being noted on the shelflist card.

NUMERIC IDENTIFIERS are specific numbers that have been attached to each edition of a title that is unique to that edition. These numeric identifiers include the ISBN (International Standard Book Number) or the LCCN (Library of Congress Card Number). *See glossary for more detail.*

CD-ROM UTILITY stands for Compact Disk-Read Only Memory Utility. CD-ROM is a very high density storage medium often used in libraries. Organizations or corporations that have large databases of cataloged titles are able to use the CD-ROM medium to make the databases available for data conversion.

Start at the beginning

You can start your inventory by taking the first tray of shelflist cards into the stacks. Since the shelflist is your book inventory record arranged in the same order as the books are arranged on the shelf, the task is fairly straight forward. You match the book on the shelf to the card in the shelflist file, and mark the book and the card to note that the book has been inventoried.

If you come to a book that does not have a shelflist card, you should remove it from the shelf to be cataloged later. If there is no cataloging available from the item or from your utility, you may wish to discard it. Review your weeding guidelines and decide whether or not to keep the item. If you discard it, you will save the cost of cataloging it now and the cost of doing the data conversion work later.

If you have a card in the shelflist file and no book on the shelf, one of several things may be true. The book may be checked out, or the book may be lost or stolen. The book may be at the bindery, or it could be shelved in the wrong place. You will want to flag (or mark) the shelflist card for the missing book, usually with a paper clip or a plastic sleeve. (Library supply companies sell plastic sleeves in a variety of colors for card catalog cards.) You will have to check the shelf later to see if the book has been returned. If it doesn't appear after a few weeks, you may need to check your circulation files, your bindery files, or your lost book files. Once you determine that the library does not have the book, you will need to remove the shelflist record and the cards from the card catalog. If you decide to replace the book, keep the cards and refile them if they match the replacement copy.

Inventory is a tedious task, but it is an essential and rewarding step in your plan to automate.

Weeding and inventory at the same time

If you want to be very efficient, you may choose to weed and do your inventory at the same time. The more operations you can conduct at the same time, the more money you will save. Get a copy of *The CREW Method*, a copy of the latest *Public Library Catalog*, a copy of *Fiction Catalog*, and a copy of the *Children's Catalog*. Make a scratch copy of the Flow Chart for Weeding a Book Collection (see appendix A). Put these tools on a book truck and go to the stacks. Take an empty book truck with you for books you remove for discard. You may want to wait until you have a "bad hair" day or some other time when you feel especially merciless. Weeding a library collection takes an attitude that is often foreign to most librarians. Every item is like a child they have brought into the world and have nurtured. To throw a book away is against normal feelings.

Take each book off the shelf and conduct the inventory procedure. Then decide if you want to keep the book. Use your scratch copy of the Weeding Flow Chart to write your own criteria for discarding a book or keeping it. Once you have your criteria in mind, don't waffle. Seriously consider discarding books that have no shelflist cards. Mark each shelf as you finish the inventory and weeding. (We use little peel and stick dots.) One pass through the collection and you are done, except for the missing books.

When you finish one shelf, say to yourself "This is the last time I will have to spend this much time doing the inventory."

Eventually the automation system will help you with the weeding and inventory process. It will help you identify which books were published over ten years ago. The system will generate a report that identifies the books that haven't been checked out for any given number of years.

Using standard catalogs

Since 1918 the H. W. Wilson Company has been publishing standard catalogs for use in libraries. Other companies have published similar collection development tools you may also find useful. These catalogs list recommended titles with brief summaries. They are indispensable to any weeding project. Unless the condition of a book makes it unacceptable to keep in the collection, any book listed in one of the standard catalogs should not be discarded.

These standard catalogs are also helpful to librarians who receive "attic gleaning" gift books. The standard catalog can help you decide if the gift book should be added to the library's collection or passed on to the book sale.

Summary

Weeding the collection and conducting an inventory are the first steps to a successful automation project. If you don't take them, you can count on spending more time and money when you automate. Get the tools you need and start. While you are working on weeding, you can begin gathering and evaluating information on automation systems. Writing for vendor information takes time. You can continue your weeding project while you are waiting for the vendor responses to come in.

Notes

1. John M. Cohn, Ann L. Kelsey, and Keith Michael Fiels. *Planning for Automation: A How-To-Do-It Manual for Librarians.* New York: Neal-Schuman, 1992.

2. List originally prepared by Donald B. Reynolds when he was the Assistant Administrator, Central Kansas System, He is now the director of the Nolichucky Regional Library, Morristown, TN.

Suggested reading

Boom, Belinda. *The CREW Method: Expanded Guidelines for Collection Evaluation and Weeding for Small and Medium-Sized Public Libraries.* Austin, Texas: Texas State Library, 1995.

Fiction Catalog, 12th ed. Edited by Juliette Yaakov and John Greenfeldt. New York: H. W. Wilson Company, 1991.

Public Library Catalog, 9th ed. Edited by Paula B. Entin and Juliette Yaakov. New York: H. W. Wilson Company, 1989.

Children's Catalog, 16th ed. Edited by Juliette Yaakov with the assistance of Ann Price. New York: H. W. Wilson Company, 1991.

Cohn, John M. Ann L. Kelsey, and Keith Michael Fiels. *Planning for Automation: A How-to-Do-It Manual for Librarians*, Neal-Schuman, 1992.

Kroll, Carol. "Preparing the Collection for Retrospective Conversion." *School Library Media Quarterly*, (Winter 1990): 82-83.

> **ATTIC GLEANINGS** are books that people give the library after they don't need them any more. Some titles are in better condition than identical titles on the library's shelves. Once in a while a librarian may miss purchasing a recommended title when it is new, but find it in a box of donated books. The standard catalogs help identify recommended titles a librarian may have missed.

Researching Automation Systems and Vendors

Chapter 3

Selecting an automation system is like choosing a marriage partner. You need to make sure you can live with your choice over the long haul. Once you commit yourself, you will have to live with the virtues or shortcomings of your partner for a long time. So the advice to "Keep your eyes wide open before marriage and half closed afterward" is still true. No automation system is totally perfect. They all have flaws. However, they are so much better than any manual system that I know of no librarian who has automated a library and wanted to go back to a manual system.

What should the automation system do?

Once you have decided to automate your library, you will need to select which library functions you want automated. Begin meeting with the board, the staff, and interested citizens to ask them what it is they want the automation system to do. I cannot over emphasize the importance of involving the staff and the board from the beginning. Tell your board or administration that you want to automate the library, and ask for permission to develop a plan and select the software. Most staff members will welcome the opportunity to automate the library, and you'll want to maintain their support by involving them as much as possible in the project.

Then, and only then, begin your search for a library automation system. Promise yourself that you will look until you find the best system for your library. Don't settle for less. The inferior quality of a less expensive product will endure long after the attractiveness of its lower price has faded. On the other hand, you have to be realistic. If you can only afford $30,000 to automate, don't expect to buy a system that will cost over $100,000.

Automation modules

Library automation systems come in modules like expensive stereo systems, with amplifiers, turntables, tape and CD players, speakers, etc. Automating a small library will require only the basic modules. The most common library

> **AUTOMATION MODULES** are a major program or function in an automated library system. For example, an automated system may consist of a circulation module, an online module and a cataloging module. They are called integrated if they are connected through the software and work together.

automation modules include circulation, public access catalog, and cataloging. Functions with these modules include overdue notices, reports, bibliographies, and inventory. The library automation package may be able to do some things you have never thought of before.

A major question in selecting a library automation system is: How well will it meet your needs in the future? Results take time to measure. A system that meets your needs today may not work so well ten years from now. If the company fails to support the system you select after five years, what will it take to switch to a different system? Will your bar codes still work? Will you be able to move your bibliographic records to a new system? These are just a few of the questions you need to ask yourself before making a commitment to a company to use their software in your library. You could be consummating a long-term marriage, and a divorce might be painful. Be very careful! Especially if you are only trying to save a few hundred dollars. As you gather information about the various systems, you will want to consider and compare the items in the features checklist below.

Features checklist

Cost

The Murphy's Law that states "Everything costs more than it costs" is absolutely true when it comes to automating a library. There will always be something that you didn't think of or didn't know about. Something you realize you absolutely have to have that you didn't plan for. You can protect yourself from this phenomenon by adding fifteen percent to the total budgeted cost of the project for contingencies.

Some systems will charge you for the software and then charge you a licensing fee based on the number of computers you plan to have in your network. Others will charge you a flat fee for the software and allow you to have unlimited access points. This issue could be a deciding factor if cost is very important to you.

The Great Bend Public Library could not afford the larger Unix or mainframe-based systems. We selected a personal computer-based system that works well with a Pentium file server. All of the systems we considered were in the $3,000 to $10,000 range for the network version. This is the same price range we have used for this book.

MARC Records

MARC stands for **MA**chine **R**eadable **C**ataloging and is the standard for all bibliographic data in libraries. The Library of Congress originally developed the MARC system to distribute its cataloging more efficiently. By creating shared bibliographic records in a standard format that can be used in many different computer systems, MARC spares librarians many hours of original cataloging and tedious retyping every time a new item is added to the library's collection.

MARC Records represent shared cataloging information, but they have the flexibility to adapt to local libraries. Local information can be added to them, and data fields can be rearranged without retyping the entire record. The system you select should be able to import and export full MARC

Standard Automation Modules:

Acquisitions & Book Fund Accounting

Bar Code Generation

Cataloging

Circulation

Community Information & Calendar

Equipment Scheduling

Fines

Online Catalog

Overdue Notification

Patron Registration & Files

Reserve Check Out

Serials Control & Accounting

UNIX is a multi-user and multi-tasking operating system originally developed by AT&T. It has become increasingly popular because it is structured in a fashion that makes it easier to operate on many different types of computers on the same network. Unix is the operating system of choice when designing open systems.

IMPORT/EXPORT
Transferring bibliographic records from another source to your database is referred to as importing data. Transferring data from your database to another database is referred to as exporting data. If a system does not support importing and exporting of full MARC records, it may be impossible to move bibliographic records from one automation system to another without losing data.

records. If you have to change vendors, and your system does not support the import and export of MARC records, you could end up re-keying your entire collection again.

Windows versus DOS

MS-DOS (or DOS, which refers to the same thing) has been the operating system for many IBM-compatible computers for several years. Library automation software that runs under Windows is on the leading edge of technology for libraries today. Most of the systems we surveyed, though not all, use the Windows 3.1 or Windows 95 platform. It is more user-friendly than DOS because of its graphical user interface and on-screen helps. Windows 95 appears destined to become the industry standard, though subsequent releases may be worth waiting for. Although DOS computers and software will probably be in use for several more years, I believe that selecting a DOS-based automation system would be taking a step backwards. Patrons will expect to see Windows on computers at the library.

A true benefit of a Windows-based automation system is the ability to use hypertext searching capabilities. Hypertext searching is an especially powerful tool. If you want to find other titles by the same author, other books in a series, or more specific topics within a subject, you can highlight the keyword or phrase and find the same keyword or phrase in other records.

Another reason for using Windows is the Internet. Current Internet software depends on graphics extensively and this promises to be more important in the future.

This discussion of DOS versus Windows might be unnecessary except that some vendors of small systems are still not moving to a Windows environment. Until they do the point is worth mentioning. Strictly DOS computers are all but obsolete and so is DOS-based software.

Compatibility

Some public libraries may seriously consider a system that is already in use in the local school. This is a valid consideration since a lot of public library use comes from students, and student users would already be familiar with the system. Public librarians may be able to allow students to use the same borrower card they get at school.

Depending on the system selected, you may also be able to share bibliographic data files with the school. For instance, some systems will allow you to establish multiple collections on the same system. In that case the collection from the school could be imported as a separate collection. It could be searched from the public library's online catalog, even though public library patrons will not be able to find these books in the library.

On the other hand, the school may be using a system that is now obsolete. If that is true, the decision-makers in the public library should have the confidence to move ahead on their own and select the system that best matches their own criteria. A lot depends on how closely the school and the public library are cooperating. If they don't cooperate very much now, chances are that selecting compatible systems will do little to raise the level of cooperation.

GRAPHICAL USER INTERFACE is an interface delivered by the computer's operating system that allows the user to select commands by using a pointing device such as a mouse.

HYPERTEXT is a software system that links text to other text or pictures. It allows for searching a word or phrase within a bibliographic record. Patrons or librarians can search the database for a word or phrase found in one record and find the occurrence of the word or phrase in all other records in the database.

COMPATIBILITY:
1) the ability of a computer to run software and/or use peripherals designed for another computer,

2) the ability of all components of an automated system to work together in a harmonious and mutually supporting fashion.

Industry and national standards for bar codes

The system should support industry standard bar codes and non-proprietary bar code readers. Bar codes are nearly universal today. The Universal Product Code is perhaps most responsible for increasing public awareness of bar coding. In libraries bar coding has not reached the same level of universality as the Universal Product Code, but it would behoove librarians who are considering automation to become aware of the trend toward an industry standard for library bar coding. Diane Peterson a marketer for Graphic Technology Inc., a major producer of bar code labels for industrial use and libraries, explains the use of standard bar codes, "Code 39 has been the accepted industry standard. Within the last year Code 128 is being pushed into that position, but not in libraries—which seem to stay with Code 39 or CODABAR. Code 39 is still very heavy into the industrial market places."

My advice would be to use Code 39, Code 128 or CODABAR for bar code symbology. They all include bi-directional decoding and character self-checking. If you buy bar code labels from the library automation vendor, *find out whether or not their bar codes can be read by other systems*, not if their bar code readers can read other bar codes.

Some systems offer software programs that let you create your own bar codes. This is okay if they can be read by other systems or if they use Code 39, Code 128 or CODABAR symbology. I recommend purchasing preprinted bar code labels that follow industry standards. Depending on the quantities ordered, you can purchase them for between $20 and $35 per thousand, plus a one-time set up charge. The cost for 10,000 preprinted dumb bar code labels would be about $450; this is about what you would pay for a software program that would let you print your own labels. Pre-printed labels can be used with any system. Depending on the symbology used, bar codes created in-house may or may not work with other systems.

Proprietary bar code readers work with only one automation system. The supplier puts their own computer chip in the readers to make them work with their automation system. If you change systems and have proprietary bar code readers, you will have to buy new bar code readers.

Searching capabilities

An automation system should have powerful searching capabilities in all modules. One of the advantages of having an automation system is the ability to search the database by more than just the first word of a title, author, or subject heading. The online catalog module should offer a simple and easy to understand interface for finding items in the library. The program should be simple enough to allow grade-school children to find what they want in the library. At the same time the system should be sophisticated enough to allow the serious researcher pinpoint access to the collection. The system should provide Boolean or combined search capabilities. Boolean "and" searching allows words to be combined within one field, or across fields. The Boolean "or" logic can be used to limit searches. Boolean "not" logic is used to streamline the search by eliminating terms.

Some systems use indexes in combination with Boolean searching. For example a patron wants to find a video on cake decorating that was published in 1995. She could start with the format index and input "video," then select

NON-PROPRIETARY BAR CODE READERS have not been modified to read only a certain automation system's bar codes. They are universal bar code readers that can read any standard bar code.

BI-DIRECTIONAL BAR CODES can be read from either direction. This is important when you want to check-in or check-out large batches of books or when you do the inventory.

One of the libraries in the Central Kansas Library System supplies books to a local school. While the school library is automated, their system cannot read our bar codes. They have to put one of their bar code labels on each of our books to check them out.

BOOLEAN SEARCHING is a powerful searching method offered in the more sophisticated online catalogs. It uses the terms "and," "or," and "not" to narrow or broaden a search.

the subject index and type "cake decorating," and finally she would select the publication date index and enter "1995." The system would find the exact item or items the patron wanted. Using the same technique another patron could get a list of all the videos owned by the library in which John Wayne appeared.

Sophisticated automation systems allow you to search any field in the database. You need that capability from the circulation, public catalog, and cataloging modules. With this capability, a patron can call and ask for an obscure title or have incomplete information and you will still find the material by using superior search capabilities.

You will want to remember, it is not enough just to try the system under ideal circumstances. You have to test it in a way that will show you how it works when words are misspelled or other important pieces of information are missing.

Ease of use

The system should be designed for ease of use by nontechnical personnel and patrons. Patrons should be able to walk up to a public access computer and type in a word or phrase and press <Enter> to begin a search. At this point they should get a response that will help them find what they are looking for, even if they spell the word incorrectly. After they press <Enter>, patrons should see a list of books with their authors and call numbers. If they find a book they want on the list, they should be able to select the title, press <Enter> and see more information about the book. The display should show the call number in about the same place it appears on a card in the card catalog. Patrons should also be able to find out if the book is on the shelf or checked out. They should be able to create a bibliography or a reading list from their computer search and then be able to print it out.

Patrons want something easy to understand when they use the library. They understand the card catalog, but many of them still need help finding what they want. An automated system will not change that, but the system you select could make a difference. If you can find a system that has screens to prompt users through the search process, so much the better.

While for ease of use it is desirable to have a system with an opening screen that says, "Type a word or phrase and press <Enter>." You may also want to have search capabilities that use more sophisticated strategies. Boolean or combined word searches will help patrons get more specific when they need to.

The best way to find out if a system is easy to use is to get some hands-on time with it. Some vendors will send you a sample program with limited records and borrowers loaded on the database. If you can't get a sample disk, then go to a library that uses the system you are considering and spend some time becoming acquainted with it. I would not buy a system that I didn't have a chance to try.

Support service

Good technical support is being able to call a toll-free number and talk with a real person who will help solve your problem the first time you call. Bad support is calling for help and reaching only an answering machine, then receiving a response in a day or two after having left an urgent request for help.

When we took staff members from the Great Bend Public Library to see other systems, each one of us had our own misspelled word to check out. Some systems were better than others at getting us to the material we wanted, even when we misspelled the main word like "dinasaur."

The best way to determine the speed of the response and the quality of technical support is to call current customers of the company.

When you call other librarians, ask them about their experiences with technical support. Don't just rely on the list of libraries the vendor representative gives you. Try to find additional libraries that are using the same system whose experiences may have been different.

> **You are better off relying on the experiences of current customers than the promises of sales representatives when comparing support services.**

> ### Questions to ask other librarians about their technical support.
>
> How often have you had to call your library automation company for technical support?
>
> What are some of the specific problems you have had?
>
> From the time you placed the call, how long did it take to get an answer that solved your problem?
>
> Was the solution something you could have figured out by reading the manual?

If you find a librarian who is not satisfied with the software vendor, be careful not to blame all of the complaints on the software company. Some of the libraries we visited had major problems, but their problems were not all related to the software. Some had to deal with electrical problems that were beyond the control of the software vendor. Others had some training problems that kept them from being totally successful.

Personnel considerations for system maintenance

Regardless of the system you select, you will need someone on staff to run the automation system. This person will be in charge of calling for support services from the automation vendor. He or she will also be in charge of doing the backups and loading the new software releases. This person doesn't have to be a computer genius. He or she just needs to know more about computer software than anyone else on the staff. The ease of use of the system and quality technical support will be very important to the head of your technology team.

System security

The purpose of system security is to prevent accidental or unauthorized modification to records. It should include safeguards that make it impossible to erase or change a record from a patron terminal. It should also allow library personnel to create overdue notices that retain the privacy of individuals, once materials have been checked in.

The system should provide safeguards against unauthorized access to the system for each module. You don't want patrons getting into circulation records and erasing fines they owe. Nor do you want them to mess with your online catalog—libraries have experienced very expensive losses when computer enthusiasts have entered their systems and erased thousands of bibliographic records. System security should be the best you can afford.

The system should provide for passwords for each major function and menu items. The system administrator should be able to create and change passwords as necessary, and do it easily without a lot of technical expertise.

Screen displays

When library patrons search the card catalog they are used to seeing biblio-graphic information displayed in a certain format. The display they see on the computer screen should replicate, as closely as possible, the format of the catalog card. The call number should appear near the top of the record. The author and title should be displayed in the upper middle of the screen. The patron shouldn't have to hunt all over the computer screen to locate this familiar information.

A card catalog can't tell you if a particular book is checked out or not. An integrated library automation system can. This is important information to the patron, and it should be visible when the patron sees the title display.

```
Copies       1

Status       On shelf

Call         220.8 Paterson

Author       Paterson, John (John Barstow); Paterson,
             Katherine.; Dowden, Anne Ophelia Todd,; 1907- ;
             ill.

Title        Consider the lilies : plants of the Bible /
             John & Katherine Paterson ; paintings by Anne
             Ophelia Dowden.

Edition      1st ed.

Subject      1. Plants in the Bible--Juvenile literature.
             2. Plants in the Bible.

Notes        Includes index.

             Bibliography: p. 94-95.

             Presents botanical illustrations of familiar
             and exotic flowers, trees, and plants men-
             tioned in the accompanying Bible verses and
             selections.

Publisher    New York : Crowell, ©1986.

ISBN/ISSN    0690044615 : $11.95 0690044631 (lib bdg.) :
             $11.89

LCCN          85043603 /AC

Phys Desc    96 p. : col. ill. ; 25 cm.
```

Figure 3.1: Sample Screen Layout from Online Catalog.

The best way to decide if the screen display of a particular software package will work for your library is to try several systems. If the company will send you a demonstration disk, load it and "play" with it for a while. Try to think like your patrons think. Invite one or two library customers to try it out. If they need a lot of coaching or instruction, other patrons may have some of the same difficulties. If they can maneuver their way around the program and find what they want, you may have a winner.

Another way to get hands-on access is to visit a library that already has the software installed. Try to put yourself in the place of a patron, or better yet, take a board member or a student with you.

You are also looking for simplicity. You don't want your patrons to look at a screen that is complicated. I prefer an opening screen that tells the patron to type a word or phrase and press <Enter>. They shouldn't have to know whether they want to search by author, title or subject. Windows-based software has a user-friendly graphical interface. The screens may not contain as much information as DOS-based systems do, but the screen displays are much easier to read.

Circulation module

One of the main reasons you install a library automation system is to check out books and keep track of borrowers and overdue materials. Here are a few things you will probably want the system to do:

- Link a unique item record with a patron record for each charge transaction and store the transaction on the computer.

- Include an inventory function.

- Make it easy for the library to comply with privacy rules.

- Flag materials that can't be checked out.

- Flag materials already checked out to another patron.

- Flag materials on reserve for another patron.

- Provide mechanisms for collecting circulation statistics and printing reports.

- Display circulation status information in the online public access catalog without revealing the identity of patrons.

- Provide a component for reserving materials or placing holds.

- Allow authorized staff to manually override all hold processing.

- Produce overdue notices and fine notices.

- Allow for specification of a fine schedule that levies no fine or fees for certain types of materials or classes of patrons.

- Check patron status and signal exceptional conditions such as excessive number of books charged, excessive fines, expired patron IDs, and excessive items claimed to be returned.

Another critical question is: How easy is it to move from the circulation function to another function? You may be checking out some books to a patron when she asks, Do you have the latest Danielle Steel novel? You need to be able to switch to the online catalog seamlessly to search for the title. A single key stroke or the click of the mouse should be all you need to do to move from the circulation function to the search function and back again.

Report features

For years library suppliers produced circulation record books that kept track of circulation by Dewey classes. Some librarians collected the data, but rarely used it. Today we generally keep circulation statistics by fiction and nonfiction, juvenile and adult. We also keep track of year-to-date statistics and compare them to last year's figures.

Your automation system will be able to give you reports that you may never have thought of before.

> You will be able to know which subjects in your collection are frequently used and make some collection development decisions based on usage.

> You will be able to determine the last time a book was checked out and use that information for weeding.

> You may be able to match certain patron types to collection usage and use the information to meet their needs.

> You will be able to determine how much money you spent on certain areas of the collection and then track how much usage was made of those materials.

Automation systems can generally produce more reports than most librarians can use. The trick is deciding which reports are most relevant and useful.

Here are some reporting features you may want the system to have:

Provide online statistical reports.

Provide statistical reports for circulation activities (on a daily basis) that can be cumulated for a month or a year.

Provide the following statistical reports:
> Number of materials by type.
> Number of patrons by type.
> Usage per month by material type.
> Total check-outs to date.
> Total fines paid to date.

Generate data for the following reports:
> Patrons with expired cards.
> Deleted patron bar code numbers.
> Patron records with messages.

Generate 4x6 inch postcards for overdue notices.

Developing a comparison matrix

You probably want to develop your own matrix similar to the one that follows in figure 3.2. Start by listing the features that are important to you and then list the top four or five systems you select across the top. If any of the systems lack features you need, eliminate them from consideration right away.

The Great Bend Public Library receives an Interlibrary Loan Development Grant each year to enhance the library's ability to cope with interlibrary loan demands. With our automation system we can track the use of the books purchased with these funds and tell how many went out to other libraries.

Make sure you request information from the automation vendors.
Every software vendor we requested information from sent thick packets of materials. Most of it promoted their software, but much of it was general information about automation that was valuable regardless of the automation system being considered.

Questions to ask in comparing automation system features	System A	System B	System C
How much will the automation software cost for our library?			
Can the system import and export full MARC records?			
Does the system use a Windows-based interface?			
Is the system compatible with other systems used in the area?			
Are the bar codes the system uses compatible with other systems?			
Are the bar code readers compatible with other bar code readers?			
Do the bar codes this system uses match industry standards? (Code 39, Code 128, or CODABAR)			
Does the system's security system provide password protection from accidental or intentional changes to the database by unauthorized personnel?			
Are the screen displays easy to use with little or no instruction?			
Is important information displayed in familiar locations? e.g., Is the call number where you would expect to see it?			
Is the circulation module easy to use?			
Can you move from the circulation function to the search function quickly and easily?			
Does the system include an inventory function?			
Does the system erase the links between the borrower and the material borrowed once the item has been checked in?			
Does the system flag materials that cannot be checked out?			
Does the system flag materials already checked out or on reserve to another patron?			
Does the system flag patrons with overdue items or outstanding fines?			
Does the system provide mechanisms for collecting circulation statistics and generating reports?			
Does the system provide a component for reserving materials or placing holds?			
Does the system allow authorized staff to manually override holds and flags for overdues?			
Does the system calculate fines and record payments automatically?			
Can the system produce overdue and fine notices?			
Does the system allow for specification of a fine schedule that is different for different material types and patron groups?			
Can the system provide a report on the titles a patron has checked out?			
Does the system signal for exceptional conditions such as excessive books checked out, excessive fines, expired patron card, or excessive items claimed returned?			

Figure 3.2: Automation System Comparison Chart.

Interviewing other librarians

One of the best ways to learn about a particular brand of automation software is to ask other librarians who are using it. The *American Library Directory* (New York: Bowker) lists the automation equipment used by libraries, and it is a good place to start. Before you call anyone remember these two points:

1. Any automation system is so much better than a manual system that regardless of whom you may ask about their automation system, they will probably be very positive when comparing it to no automation at all.

2. The librarians you speak with probably took some time and energy to select the system they are using and have some of themselves invested in its success. They may be slow to admit that they are not entirely happy with their selection.

Before you pick up the telephone and start calling, you will probably want to develop a set of questions you will ask everyone.

Here are a few questions you might consider:

Questions to ask other librarians about their automation systems.

Which automation systems did you consider before making your final choice?

What were the deciding factors that caused you to select the system you are using?

Have you discovered anything about this system that you didn't know before you bought it?

Would these discoveries have caused you to select another system had you known them earlier?

What do you like best about your system?

What do you wish it could do that it doesn't do?

How responsive has the company been to suggestions to improve the system?

Have new releases to the software been a dream or a nightmare?

When something goes wrong with the software, what do you do and how long does it take for support services to respond?

If you could go back to a point when you were selecting the software for your automation project, would you have selected another brand of software?

Is there anything you would have done differently, including data conversion, hardware selection, or implementation?

Summary

This has been a brief summary of some points to consider when you select a library automation system. You want to be happy with your choice for years to come. The choices you make will be based on the answers you get to important questions. Your questions will be based on the priorities you set. If one of your priorities is to have a system like the school has, you may have to accept answers you don't like in some other areas.

Ask lots of questions. Talk to several vendors. Call librarians that already have the systems you are considering. Find out the strengths and weaknesses of their system. Go for an on-site visit if you can. Involve the board and the staff in this process. Most of all, don't settle for a library automation system that you see in a catalog or promotional flyer—just because it is within your price range. Check it out thoroughly before you make a commitment. Get some hands-on experience with it. The cost of the automation software will be minimal compared to other costs you will incur. Once you make your selection, move ahead with confidence.

Suggested readings

Breeding, Marshall, "Athena: A Windows-Based Integrated Library System from Nichols Advanced Technologies," *Library Software Review*, (Spring 1995): 42-58.

Burkhalter, Jaque. "Help! I Just Bought a Library Automation System. Now What Do I Do?" *Library Talk*, (September/October 1993): 7-9.

Library Automation Workbook. Carlsbad, California: Data Trek, 1992.

McElmeel, Sharon L. "Welcome to an Automated Library." *Library Talk*, September/October 1993: 1+.

Murphy, Catherine, ed. *Automating School Library Catalogs: A Reader*. Englewood, Colorado: Libraries Unlimited, 1992.

Pitkin, Gary M., ed. *Library Systems Migration: Changing Automated Systems in Libraries and Information Centers*. Westport, Connecticut: Meckler, 1991.

Researching the Computer Hardware

Chapter 4

The key decision you need to make about hardware for your library is really one of quantity. How many computers do you need to serve your staff and patrons? What will your budget allow?

The range of choices you have falls into three basic configurations:

1. **Stand-Alone System** with one computer (see figure 4.1).

2. **Peer-to-Peer Network** using from two to eight computers (see figure 4.2)

3. **Client-Server Network** for more than eight computers (see figure 4.3).

The configuration you select will depend on the needs of your library and your patrons. Whatever you do, I suggest that you keep your options open for expansion because public demand for computers is growing faster than most librarians think it is.

Stand-Alone System

If your library's automation needs can be met with a single personal computer, you probably can use a stand-alone system. A stand-alone system means that all functions—cataloging, circulation, and public access catalog—will be done on one computer. A very small or highly specialized library may have only a few patrons a day—rarely will there be more than one or two people in the library at a time. They may only need to search the OPAC occasionally. Circulation may be limited to less than one hundred per day. If this sounds like your library you may not need a network.

Even if more than one computer is required, you may still be able to get by without a network. The large storage capabilities of CD-ROMs can provide access to a great deal of data. If you have an Internet connection, one computer can give access to more information than you may ever need.

Indeed, my vision for the very small library of the future is a well-managed collection of less than 10,000 books for light reading and current information, and a fast connection to the Internet. This small library will be able to compete with the larger library having hundreds of thousands of volumes.

Patti Steiben, the librarian in Otis, Kansas, (population 365) has automated her library with a stand-alone system. She says, "It was a lot of work to get all the books on the computer, but it was worth it." The library only has about 3,000 books, and it took Patti about a year, working a few hours every day, to add the collection to the automation database.

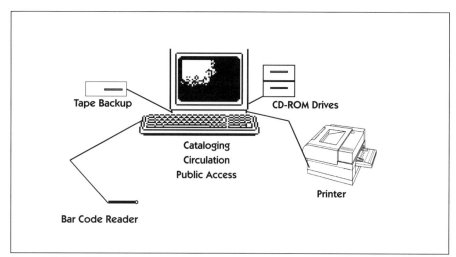

Figure 4.1: Stand-Alone System

A **STAND-ALONE SYSTEM** is a single computer used for automation. It is not connected to another computer. All library functions (cataloging, searching and circulation) are performed on the same computer.

But it may not be for you

A stand-alone system may not be for everyone. If you want your public access catalog to display the shelf status of any item in the library; or if you need multiple checkout locations; or if your cataloging cannot be done on the same workstation you use for other functions, you may need to set up a network.

Laura Einstadter of Bellingham (Massachusetts) Public Library started out with a stand-alone system and wasn't happy with it. She said, "I would not go with a stand-alone system. I would have thought more towards the future and installed an online network. Although a stand-alone system is better than nothing, I would still opt for a networked system."

Networking Options

Peer-to-Peer Network

The smallest hardware and network configuration I can recommend is a peer-to-peer network that uses no fewer than three computers—though it is possible to get by with only two computers (see figure 4.2). This configuration will work well for a library with up to 50,000 titles; 10,000 borrowers and up to eight work stations. If this configuration is too small for your library, you can build on the plan and make it larger to meet your needs.

A peer-to-peer network uses the computing and storage power of all the computers on the network. The computer you use for cataloging may have a larger hard drive because it will house the entire database. However, most computers purchased today come with plenty of hard disk storage for applications for a small peer-to-peer network.

Client-Server Network

A library with more borrowers and books may want to use a file server in a client-server environment. The file server is linked to a central concentrator that distributes signals to and from each of the work stations (see figure 4.3).

The **file server** is a powerful microcomputer that usually has more computing power and more storage capacity than the other computers on the

A **CONCENTRATOR** is a device used to join communications channels from several different network nodes or segments. It is like a traffic cop standing in the middle of an intersection directing traffic. You need one of these whenever you connect two or more computers together in a network.

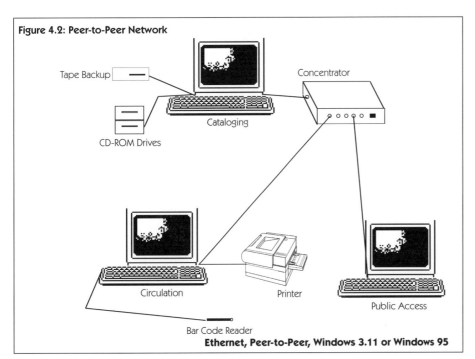

Figure 4.2: Peer-to-Peer Network

Tape Backup

Concentrator

Cataloging

CD-ROM Drives

Circulation

Printer

Public Access

Bar Code Reader

Ethernet, Peer-to-Peer, Windows 3.11 or Windows 95

PEER-TO-PEER NETWORK in which the computing and storage power of all the computers on the network is shared.

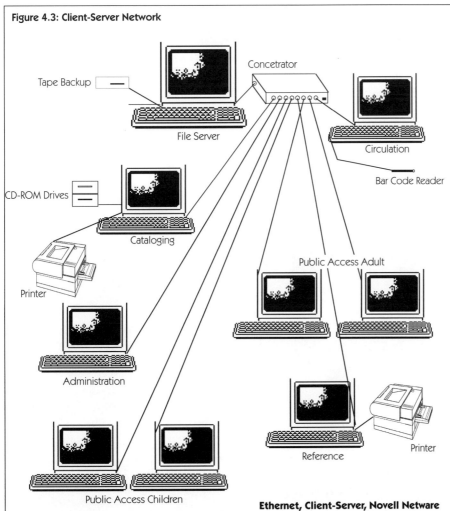

Figure 4.3: Client-Server Network

Tape Backup

Concetrator

File Server

Circulation

Bar Code Reader

CD-ROM Drives

Cataloging

Public Access Adult

Printer

Administration

Reference

Printer

Public Access Children

Ethernet, Client-Server, Novell Netware

CIIENT-SERVER NETWORK which uses a designated file server as host for all the automation software and data files.

network because it serves as the host for all of the automation software and data files. Its special use and configuration means it cannot also be used as a workstation. The file server's purpose is to pass data and software commands back and forth between other computers on the network.

While you may be able to use the computer you bought a few years ago as part of your automation network, I recommend buying the most up-to-date computers you can afford. Your automation system will be outmoded soon enough without using your old computers. If you already have a computer and you feel that it can still be put to good use, turn it into a single-use workstation for the public to use as a word processor, for CD-ROMs, or for Internet access. Don't try to attach every computer application you can think of to your automation system. Sometimes stand-alone, single purpose computers work better than if the same computer was connected to a network.

Developing a network

The computers

When you develop your network, start with a powerful computer with lots of memory and hard disk storage, a Pentium processor with 16 megabytes of RAM and 1,000 megabytes (a gigabyte) of hard disk storage. This is the computer you will use for storing the automation program and the database. Add two more computers to the network with about the same computing power and RAM. Use one for circulation and store all of the borrower files on it. Use the other computer for public access to the catalog. You will need a network card for each computer to allow you to connect them all together (see figure 4.3).

The network

To create the network, all the computers will be connected to a concentrator, like spokes on a wheel, using 10 Base-T UTP Cable. (10 Base-T UTP cabling refers to the bandwidth [10 megabits per second] which determines the speed data can travel. UTP stands for untwisted pairs, see figure 4.2). This is called an Ethernet network using a peer-to-peer topology. Ethernet is the protocol for the software that controls the electronic traffic in a network. Topology simply refers to the physical configuration of a network. It defines the hardware and the means used to connect the pieces together. Both figures 4.2 and 4.3 use an Ethernet topology, but they differ in the way computing power is shared or distributed.

In a peer-to-peer configuration, the computing power is shared between all of the computers on the network. In the client-server configuration, one computer, usually more powerful and faster than the rest, is designated as the file server. All of the programs and data are loaded on this computer and all of the computers on the network rely on it for data files and its faster computing power.

Network topology is somewhat analogous to cable television. The cable company installs a cable connection in your home. This cable goes to a distribution hub where the signal is concentrated and sent to the various connec-

A GIGABYTE is approximately one billion bytes. It is used to express the capacity of disk storage.

A MEGABYTE is one million bytes. The term is often used to express the capacity of memory or disk storage. A microcomputer may come with 8 MB of RAM and a 840 MB hard disk.

A NETWORK CARD is a computer device that attaches to your computer. It has a plug-in that looks like a telephone jack. Cabling similar to telephone cable is run from the network card in the computer to the concentrator. Each computer on the network needs a network card.

RAM stands for Random Access Memory. It is the computer's internal memory chips used to store data that can be read or written to. RAM is volatile and any data in RAM are erased when the power to the computer is turned off or fails. RAM is measured in kilobytes or megabytes, e.g., 640K, 16 MB.

tions it serves. The cable company cannot have a hundred thousand individual wires, one from each home running back to the single distribution point. It uses a system of hubs to split the signal and direct it to each home.

Jeff Underwood, a technology consultant (Great Bend, KS) who has set up automation networks in several small libraries, recommends Windows 95 in a peer-to-peer network. Windows 95 comes loaded on many new computers and has more than adequate networking capabilities for networks with up to eight computers. In a larger network he recommends Windows NT 3.51, which is designed for a file server environment because it can be installed without changing the peer-to-peer topology.

Network software

Also analogous to the cable connection is the software. You can be connected to the cable, but if the cable company doesn't send the television signal out, you won't get it on your television set. Just as you need library automation software to circulate books, you need networking software to direct the electronic signals between computers on your network. Most new computers now come with Windows 95, which includes networking software. This network will accommodate up to about ten computers. It will work with more than that, but possibly not as well. If you plan to connect more than ten computers to your network, you may want to consider using a file server and Novell Netware (see figure 4.2).

Bar code readers

Add a bar code reader to the circulation computer and one to the cataloging computer, and you have the basis for your automation network. When bar code readers scan or read a bar code, the bar code is translated to a number and the number appears on the computer screen in the field you have selected. CCD scanners are somewhat easier to use, but light pens are less expensive and perform the same function. If you want to save money, buy a light pen. If you can, try them both before you decide.

Printers

Attach a printer to one of the computers—I recommend the circulation computer—then add the cabling between the computers and the concentrator, and your basic network is complete. If you are using Windows 95 over an Ethernet network, any of the computers will be able to access the printer. All of this hardware can be purchased for about $7,000.

Backups

Because you will spend thousands of dollars to set up the network and lots of time on data conversion, you really need a tape backup unit to protect your data in case the hard disk crashes. The backup can be programmed to do its job automatically. Someday you will be glad you have your backup tape.

BAR CODE READERS come in two varieties, CCD (Charged Coupled Device) and light pens. They are connected to the computer between the key board and the CPU (Central Processing Unit).

CENTRAL PROCESSING UNIT (CPU) is the main component of a microcomputer. It functions as the brain of the computer, executing and managing all the computer functions.

A LIGHT PEN is a device resembling a pen that is connected to the computer and is used to optically identify or read an item or patron bar code.

NOVELL NETWARE is the networking software of choice for larger networks. Pricing is based on the number of users on the network.

WINDOWS 95 is an operating system from the Microsoft Corporation. Its graphical user interface makes it easier for users to access files and work with them. Included with this operating system is good, though limited, networking software. Depending on the traffic, it can handle eight to ten computers connected to a network.

Watch for rapid changes in technology

The hardware recommendations here should be considered as examples only. By the time you read this book, newer, faster hardware will be available. Most of the automation software you consider will run on older computers. And while you want your hardware to last as long as possible, you also need to count on replacing most of it every five to ten years.

I recommend that you purchase hardware from a local vendor if they offer a competitive price and will provide hardware maintenance at a reasonable cost. Some small towns don't have local vendors, so you need to have a local person who is well qualified to install the computers and the networking.

I have found that some factory-direct computers are a good buy, offering high performance and a good warranty at a very reasonable price. Mail order may be a good option if you can find a computer networking consultant who is willing to service your system when it fails to function. I also recommend that you contract with your library automation company for software support and maintenance.

Basic hardware and installation

FILE SERVER: If you decide to use a file server, it should be able to handle the computing needs of the system for years to come. I recommend a Pentium processor with at least 16 megabytes of RAM and one gigabyte of hard disk storage. You should also have an uninterrupted power supply and a good surge protector to safeguard your data in the event of a power outage or power surge.

You can use the file server as a stand-alone computer for your data conversion provided it has two CD-ROM drives, for the MARC record utility and data conversion. After you connect the rest of the computers to the network, it would be best not to use the file server as a workstation. Using it as a workstation will slow down all computers on the network.

WORKSTATIONS   In a minimum configuration you will need individual computer workstations for cataloging, circulation, and for the public access catalog. These workstations don't have to be as powerful as the file server, but you don't want to buy equipment that has been obsolete for years.

BAR CODE READERS   Buy these from the automation software vendor you select. That is the best way to guarantee that they will work with the software you are going to use. Be careful though; some vendors put their own computer chip in their bar code readers to make them work with their software. If you ever decide to change to another library automation software vendor, you will have to buy new bar code readers.

PRINTERS   You will need at least one printer for reports and overdue notices. Windows-based software works better with printers that are designed to handle graphics. Ink jet and laser printers are now very reasonable. You may want to have a receipt-type slip printer that can produce a printout of books that a patron has just borrowed.

LOCAL AREA NETWORK AND CABLING Each computer on the network will need a network card. This card allows the computers to talk to each other. Though there are many configurations for computer networks, I recommend an Ethernet network that uses Novell Netware. This topology requires a concentrator. This device distributes the signal to and from the file server (see figure 4.2). I recommend 10 base-T as the wiring distribution using Class 5 UTP (untwisted pairs) with keyed RJ-45 jacks.

You will have at least one network cable attached to each computer. You cannot just run the cables across the floor. You will have to run them up in the ceiling or under the floor. If you run them up in the ceiling, be aware that fluorescent light can adversely affect the computer signal if the cable is too close to the light fixture. If necessary you can run the cabling in the walls or through walls, but putting new wiring in an existing wall is costly.

Ethernet is a very mature protocol developed by Xerox, offering stability and reliability. Most newly created networks today use the Ethernet protocol.

When you solicit bids it would be wise to include the file server, the workstations, the printers, and the local area network and cabling in one bundle. As much as possible, you should define exactly what you want in each component so that all bidders are bidding on the same thing.

ELECTRICAL SUPPLY Most libraries built more than a decade ago do not have enough electrical circuits or outlets. You cannot ignore the possibility of this weakness. It would be great if every computer could run off its own circuit, but this ideal may not be possible. If your library was built in two stories, it will be relatively easy to add new electrical circuits wherever you need them. If you are not so well blessed, you may have to call in an electrical consultant to help figure out how to get electricity to the computers. Before calling an electrician, you need to decide where you are going to put each computer. Take a floor plan of the library, indicate where the current electrical circuits are, and then determine where you need new ones. Make sure you don't have to drill through 18" of concrete to put in a new line.

INSTALLATION AND TRAINING Installation of the hardware and cabling should be included in the bid. Installation of the software should be easy enough that no on-site installation should be required. You may need someone to coach you over the telephone.

Training on the network should come from the provider. You will want to provide as much hands-on training as possible, since this will be the most effective way for staff to learn the system. Once they have learned the basic system, there is on-screen help available in Windows that will answer questions as they come up.

MAINTENANCE AND SUPPORT Your hardware dealer should offer a plan to provide hardware maintenance. The company may offer a fixed rate for all components they install or an hourly rate. Either way, you need to know how the maintenance plan is set up and then budget for it.

Software support is so critical that you may decide to select a software vendor on the level and quality of support they offer. I would certainly include software support in the questions I asked librarians with automated

KEYED RJ-45 JACKS are a special type of connector that looks like standard telephone connectors. One end fits into a receptacle in the computer's network card or the concentrator. Keyed jacks have a special channel in the receptacle and a key that fits the channel on the other half of the connector. This keeps the computer network from being confused with a telephone line connection.

In Great Bend we set up a computer with a bar code reader for the circulation staff while the data conversion was in progress. The staff gave themselves new borrower cards and checked out books to each other. By the time the circulation mode was ready for the public the staff knew how to use it.

libraries. I can also assure you there is a difference between vendors, so it's important to include questions about support when talking with both vendors and other librarians about system software. There is nothing more frustrating than calling for support and leaving a message, only to be called back two or three days later.

> **Buy the fastest computers with the most RAM and storage capacity you can afford. Developing software continues to demand faster speeds.**

Personnel considerations

Even though you may have someone on staff who is in charge of the automation system, you may want to have someone available with extensive hardware knowledge, too. This is easier said than done. Most library staff members don't work with hardware enough to be experts. In a small library, you probably can't afford a full-time computer hardware expert. The next best thing is a hardware consultant across the street from the library. The problem is they usually charge $30 to $50 an hour. Or you may be able to secure a maintenance contract with someone to take care of hardware problems.

Plan for furniture

You may be able to use the furniture you already own, but don't count on it. Computer keyboards require a special height. You might also find it necessary to adjust the height of the table and the keyboard to accommodate those patrons who are in wheelchairs. It is better to put the cost of additional furniture in your plan and not need it, than to ignore furniture and wish you had included it.

Summary

You need to keep all of your options open and look to the future. Select networking solutions that are mature and open ended. You need to be able to change and improve individual components without replacing everything. Buy the fastest computers with the most RAM and storage capacity you can afford. Developing software continues to demand faster speeds, more RAM and more storage. Even then you will probably have to replace all of your hardware every five to ten years. Just try to keep up with the pace.

Suggested readings

Guide to Wide Area Networks: A Step-by-Step Introduction. Caledonia, Minnesota: Winnebago Software Company, 1995.

Howden, Norman. *Local Area Networking for the Small Library: A How-to-Do It Manual for School and Public Librarians.* New York: Neal-Schuman, 1992.

Data Conversion

Chapter 5

Don't let anyone mislead you. Data conversion is a lot of work. It will cost more than you think and take more time than you think. Roger Carswell, the director of the Iola (Kansas) Public Library, said, "Estimate the amount of time the project will take, then double it." They did their fiction manually, in-house, but they sent their nonfiction to an outside source for data conversion.

The point is, when you bring up your online catalog for the public, you will want it to be the best that it can be—so like or not, the costs in time and money for data conversion must be handled with care.

Virginia Moore, the librarian at the middle school in Tecumseh, Kansas, did the data conversion herself over a five-year period. They had approximately 20,000 circulating items in the collection. She said, "It was not easy, but worth the time and effort." In retrospect she said that she would have insisted that data input and conversion be handled by outside sources or at least that additional personnel be hired.

Data conversion can be accomplished in a variety of ways

1. Send the shelflist out to have MARC records created and produce smart bar code labels which are then attached to the books.

2. Create smart bar code labels from a database that has been extracted from a larger database of which the library's holdings are a part.

3. Extract MARC records from a CD-ROM bibliographic utility and use dumb bar code labels. (See appendix B for a list of CD-ROM bibliographic utilities.)

4. Manually key MARC records for every book and attach dumb bar code labels.

What you decide to do will depend on:

- How many titles you have.
- How much money you can spend on data conversion.
- How accurate your shelflist is.
- How much control you want to have over the quality of your catalog.
- How much staff time you can devote to the project.
- How urgent it is to get the system up and running for the public.
- Which of all these considerations is most important to you.

If you have 10,000 books, and you don't have $4,000 to $6,000 to invest in sending your shelflist off for data conversion, you will have to consider a less expensive option or raise the money for conversion. If a clean database is important, and you want to edit your MARC records, count on spending lots of staff time on the project.

As a caution, I would suggest that you do not bring up the circulation module before data conversion is substantially complete. Adding books to the database "on the fly" at the circulation desk is a waste of staff time. Take the time to do it right the first time.

Let's take a closer look at your data conversion options.

1. Send the shelflist out for data conversion.

If you have the money and your shelflist is exceptionally accurate, this is the way to go. It is the quickest way to get your library automated and open to the public. The data conversion company will come to your library and make a microfilm copy of your shelflist, or pack up your shelflist and take it to their own location. Their staff will use a database utility to find a MARC record for each title to create a database of your library's holdings.

Some vendors will even create original MARC records if they cannot find an existing one. These vendors guarantee they will provide data conversion for one hundred percent of your collection. They can also perform authority control work after the database is created. Once this is done, they can create smart bar code labels for your books, send a tape of the database to you so you can create your own bar code labels, or send your database to a third-party vendor to have them produce smart bar code labels. You will have to select the combination of options that will work best for you.

We didn't use this option in Great Bend, primarily because we didn't have $50,000 to convert our shelflist. We also had most of our records on a database known as the Kansas Library Catalog, a Kansas union catalog produced by Auto-Graphics.

2. Create smart bar code labels from a database of which the library's holdings are a part.

If your library participates in a consortium that has been cataloging your holdings on OCLC or some other bibliographic utility for a long time, you may want to select this option. The advantage with this alternative is that your MARC records have already been created and the cost of extracting your records from a larger database is less than starting from scratch.

If your library's holdings are in a large database and you have only a few thousand records, this option may not be cost effective. On the other hand if you can cooperate with several other small libraries whose holdings are on the same database, you may be able to share some of the costs.

The next step is to create a database of just your records. At this point the vendor can either do the authority control work itself or send your data

Librarians who have sent their shelflist out for conversion say it is the only way to go. Robert Lindsley of the Alfred Bauman Public Library in West Patterson New Jersey said, "Have the retrospective conversion done by the library automation company and avoid a long length of time between conversion and project activation."

At Great Bend we had Auto-Graphics, the producer of the Kansas Library Catalog (KLC) extract our records and do the authority control work. To extract our records they had to check to see if there was a holding code for the Great Bend Public Library for every record in the KLC. We had about 80,000 records on the KLC. Auto-Graphics extracted our records and compiled them into a database for us. We had them do machine authority control work, too. Outputting the records to a tape was an additional cost. In all, it cost us about $9,000 to extract our data and have the authority control work done for 80,000 records.

out for authority control work. Without authority control, differing forms of a name can cause problems in searching the OPAC and can cause confusion for patrons. Some automated systems have an authority control file to assist staff in maintaining control of names and subjects. Most PC-based programs do not have separate authority control files.

After the authority control work is done, the data will be transferred to diskettes or a computer tape. From this tape, you can have smart bar code labels created. You may choose to have this done by someone else. If you choose to produce the labels yourself, the vendor will send the tape to you so the labels can be created as part of your data conversion work.

3. Extract MARC records from a CD-ROM bibliographic utility.

If you do not have MARC records for your collection and you cannot afford to send your shelflist out for data conversion, you may like this option. You will need a computer with two CD-ROM drives, and you will need to subscribe to one of the CD-ROM bibliographic utilities. Appendix B includes a list CD-ROM bibliographic utility vendors. Subscriptions to these services can be updated monthly or quarterly.

If the bibliographic records are not located on the CD-ROM utility, the book may be old or outdated. You will have to decide if you want to keep it in the collection or discard it. If you decide to keep it, you will need to create a MARC record yourself. Your automation system will have a template for keying in records manually.

4. Manually key MARC records.

Putting your books on the computer by hand is the choice of last resort. If you have to, you could follow the procedure outlined above but substitute the process that uses the CD-ROM utility. This is a tedious, time-consuming process. Librarians who have chosen this method to get their collections automated say that it was probably worth the effort, but they do not recommend it to others. If you can afford the cost of the computers, you will probably be able to find the money to subscribe to a bibliographic utility for your data conversion.

Not only is manual data conversion a great deal more work, but it also introduces a greater potential for errors. You may be the best typist in the world, but you will still make mistakes. One of the libraries we visited hired a contractor to manually key their records. The resulting database was loaded with typographical errors. That isn't to say that there are no mistakes on the records from CD-ROM bibliographic utilities. There are, but they are minimal.

If you think you have no alternative other than to manually enter the bibliographic records, talk with at least three librarians who have done it and listen to them. In other words, figure out another way to do it.

Generating bar code labels

After you decide whether to use dumb or smart bar code labels, you will need to decide how to produce them. Many library automation companies will sell you a software program to generate your own labels on a laser or dot matrix

---

AUTHORITY CONTROL in cataloging is the establishment of one accepted "authoritative" form of a name or subject. The authority file contains records that have the accepted forms of the names and subjects and any associated cross references.

MACHINE AUTHORITY CONTROL is done with a computer and is much less expensive than manual authority control. Manual authority control work requires that a person check the records, compare names in the file, and decide which ones to use.

Glenn Ferdman, Director of the FORE Library, a small special library in Chicago, Illinois, hired an independent contractor to help manually enter approximately 2,500 titles. However, he said that if he had it to do over he would have been more careful in the choice of authority records to save time later on clean-up of the authority file.

printer. These labels are alright if they use standard symbology that can be read by other systems. You also have to pay attention to the quality of the paper stock. How good is the adhesive? Will you have to use a label protector?

You can also have labels preprinted by the thousands. Laminated labels with extra strong adhesive do not usually require label protectors. Manufacturers will guarantee that the labels will work with any system. Have the vendor send out a sample for you to test with your system before moving your project into production. I prefer preprinted bar code labels that use a standard symbology.

Authority control

Central to the successful implementation of a library automation system is a high quality database. Conversely, nothing undermines the credibility of an automation system more than a poorly prepared database. As a rule, a library's financial investment in its database far exceeds the cost of the automation hardware and software. Your database is going to be essential to the library's mission long after the library has outgrown the present automation system. If bibliographic data is substandard or has been processed improperly, patrons and staff alike will not be able to take full advantage of the automation system.

Authority control is the only way to bring the various listings of the name "Agatha Christie" together as one in your computer database. The name may be listed several different ways in your card catalog, but it can only be listed one way in your automated catalog. This is the only way to collect all the books by Agatha Christie on one computer screen or in one search.

Subject authority control merges and updates changes that have occurred over the years into one currently accepted heading for all versions of that heading. With rapidly changing technologies and the ever changing world map, this can provide a valuable update for your system.

Librarians in large libraries are concerned about authority control because they have millions of names and subjects to manage. Librarians who have fewer than 20,000 titles probably know their collection well enough that authority control is not as important. Everyone I interviewed, even those who do authority control work, questioned the necessity of authority control work for a small collection, but I strongly encourage you to do at least some authority control work. The cost for computerized authority control work that includes name authority and subject authority will cost about five cents per record. That comes to $500 for 10,000 records—not too much money in the total scheme of automation. You need to carefully weigh the pros and cons, then decide if the cost is worth it for your collection. I believe if automation is worth doing, it is worth doing right, and authority control is doing it right.

If you are using a CD-ROM product to develop your database, you can export your compiled database to floppy disks, select a vendor and send the records out for authority control. (Each high density 3.5" floppy will hold about 1,500 records. That is seven disks for a collection of 10,000 records.) It will take about a month.

Authority control with automation software

Some automation software vendors that offer systems that run on a PC network offer authority control as part of the cataloging module. Most authority control is collection specific. It relies on authority control established for the collection. You can use the authority control function when you add or change the bibliographic information for a title. If you decide to authorize a piece of bibliographic information, the system will display the appropriate authority list and highlight the item that most closely matches the entry. You can select the highlighted item or choose another item on the list and apply the authority to the bibliographic record. You do not need to create authority lists. The system does that for you, using the bibliographic information in the collection you specify to generate various lists. If this feature is important to you, you may want to select automation software that includes it.

Summary

Whatever you decide to do about data conversion, don't settle for less than the best you can afford.

I know of a janitorial service that charges more than any of its competitors, but still has all the business it can handle. Its motto is "Meticulous attention to details." Anyone who has the responsibility to convert library records to a computer database should have the same motto—Meticulous attention to details. At the Great Bend Public Library we chose to do our own data conversion and use dumb bar codes because we wanted our online catalog to be as perfect as we could make it.

Next to the selection of the automation software, data conversion could be the most critical decision you will have to make. See appendixes B and C for companies that can help with the process.

Suggested readings

Library Database Preparation Services: A Primer. Abington, Pennsylvania: Library Technologies, Inc. 1995.

Skapura, Robert. "A Primer on Automating the Card Catalog." *School Library Media Quarterly,* (Winter 1990): 75-78.

Urrows, Henry. and Elizabeth Urrows. "Automating with Barcodes." *Computers in Libraries.* (September 1991): 51-52.

Requesting Bids

Chapter 6

Once you have a good idea about what you want to do, how you are going to do it, and what kinds of hardware and software you will need; you will want to prepare a Request for Bids (or Request for Proposal). This document will help you to develop your final proposal for presentation to your board or administration by providing firm costs for the system you have selected. The ideal plan you have in mind now, may need to change if prices end up being higher than you anticipated.

Preparing a Request for Bids

Your Request for Bids will provide potential bidders with specifications for needed hardware, software, and services. While it is impossible to expect that vendors will provide bids that can be matched exactly, item by item, you want them to be as close as possible, providing an even playing field for vendors and comparable results for your evaluation. So you will create specifications that you expect can be met. If bidders have exceptions, they should note them in their bid. These exceptions should be noted when you compare bids.

You can use the Request for Bids to gather information that will help you decide between two or more options in any of the software, hardware or conversion issues we have discussed. You may still not be sure whether to send your records out for data conversion or to do them in-house. You could request bids for both methods and use price as a deciding factor. You can also request bids on different types of bar code scanners or computers with various enhancements in order to compare costs on features that you are still considering, but may not be able to afford.

If I were to request bids for the minimal system I am proposing in *Automating Small Libraries,* this is how I would present it.

LIBRARY AUTOMATION SYSTEM
FOR THE SMALL PUBLIC LIBRARY
REQUEST FOR BID BY COMPONENT

For each of the components listed below, please describe how your system would meet the needs outlined. Tell specifically what equipment or process you propose and the advantages you feel your approach has to offer. Be brief. If it is absolutely impossible to separate two components, say so, but try to price them separately.

If you are not prepared to bid on particular components of our system please mark the points you are not bidding on with "N/B" for no bid.

LIBRARY AUTOMATION SOFTWARE

We want to be able to circulate library materials and give the public access to our online catalog, both on-site and remote through their home computers. We also want to add new titles using MARC records supplied on diskette provided by the book jobber. Include here the circulation and OPAC software and the software to interface with cataloging we receive from book jobbers. Include the cost of the automation software and licensing fees for up to 10 workstations.

    Cost for Automation Software $ _____

DATA CONVERSION

We have approximately 10,000 books. Our shelflist is not very accurate, but it is up-to-date. We plan to use a CD-ROM bibliographic utility to find MARC records that we will download to the automation software. If your company offers a comparable CD-ROM product, please describe it here and list the subscription price for a quarterly update. We plan to use dumb bar codes and put them on our books at the time we do the data conversion. Our main goal is to have an extremely accurate database before we present it to the public. Include cost for 15,000 dumb bar code labels. If you offer a turn-key data conversion process please suggest it here. Include data preparation, automated authority control, smart bar codes and creation of the database for loading on to the automated system. If you offer software for creating our own bar code labels, quote your price here.

    Cost for CD-ROM bibliographic utility. $ _____

    Cost for 15,000 dumb bar code labels $ _____

    Cost for turnkey data conversion. $ _____

    Cost for bar code software $ _____

WORKSTATIONS

We want to use three computer workstations connected in a peer-to-peer configuration. Include operating system software and license for all workstations.

Figure 6.1: Sample Request for Bids

Preferred Specifications	Your Specifications
Pentium Processor	
16 MB RAM	
Ethernet 10 base T 16 bit network adapter	
540 MB HD installed	
15" Color VGA monitor	
Keyboard	
Desktop case with 200 watts power supply	
Local bus IDE floppy/hard drive controller with 2 serial and 2 parallel ports	
Windows 95 operating software	
4X CD-ROM drive, tray type	
3.5" disk drive	

Cost for two computers as specified above. $ _____

Cost for one computer with two CD-ROM drives. $ _____

BAR CODE READERS

Please bid as options: 1) One regular light pen; and 2) One CCD scanner. We prefer a device that will work with any hardware, with any software and will read industry standard bar codes. Include connecting cables and software to interface with the system.

Cost for one standard light pen. $ _____

Cost for one CCD scanner. $ _____

Cost for one laser bar code scanner. $ _____

Our bar code readers are proprietary _____ Yes _____ No

-2

PRINTERS

We would like to have the following:

One Hewlett Packard (HP 5-L) laser printer.

    Cost $ _____

One SLIP receipt printer (Model 8000) for date
due notices.

    Cost $ _____

LOCAL AREA NETWORK

We plan to install a local area network that supports Ethernet in a peer-to-peer topology, with a main concentrator (Boca Research) with eight ports. Include hardware for this local area network. Bid software if you do not plan to use Windows 95.

    Cost for concentrator. $ _____

CABLING

Please bid this component separately. We will have three computers connected in the network with a total of 100 feet between all computers. Use Class 5 UTP cable with keyed RJ-45 connectors. Include labor and materials for this cabling. Do not include network adapters which are included with the computers

    Cost for cabling $ _____

UNINTERRUPTIBLE POWER SUPPLY

In the event of a power outage we want a device that will keep the system up for 10 minutes while we power it down safely.

    Cost of power supply. $ _____

BACKUP TAPE DRIVE

    CMS Jumbo 1400, or equivalent with three tapes.
    Cost for backup tape drive. $ _____

-3

Comparing the bids

When the bids come back, you will want to create a comparison chart or table to help you and the board compare the bids and understand the cost of your automation proposal. Not all vendors will be able to bid on all components. Hardware vendors may only want to bid on the hardware or just the computers. This can work out well as long as you don't try to use the lowest bidder for each component. For example, you will probably want to have the same company install the cabling and the local area network, even if the low bid for the cabling is from one company and the low bid for the concentrator is from another company. You might even consider a turnkey system where one company does everything including data conversion, hardware, software and anything else required to make the system work. If that is what you want, tell the bidders that in your Request for Bids.

Comparison chart

Even though you might have many more columns, your comparison chart will look something like this:

Figure 6.2: Comparison Chart for Library Automation Project

Component	A	B	C	D	E
Automation software					
Data conversion CD-ROM utility					
Dumb bar code labels					
Turnkey data conversion					
Bar code software					
Two computer workstations					
Computer workstation w/2 CDs					
Bar code reader—Light pen					
Bar code reader—CCD scanner					
Printer—Laser					
Printer—Receipt					
Concentrator for LAN					
Cabling					
Uninterruptible power supply					
Backup tape drive					

After you receive all the bids and fill in the blanks your chart could look like this.

Figure 6.3: Completed Comparison Chart for Library Automation Project

Component	A	B	C	D	E
Automation software	$3,500	$4,899	$10,000	No bid	No bid
Data conversion CD-ROM utility	500	699	875	No bid	No bid
Dumb bar code labels	496	525	575	No bid	No bid
Turnkey data conversion	4,600	5,500	6,000	No bid	No bid
Bar code software	450	N/A	395	No bid	No bid
Two computer workstations	N/A	4,500	3,950	3,150	2,960
Computer workstation w/2 CDs	N/A	5,000	4,398	3,350	3,111
Bar code reader—Light pen	397	457	376	No bid	No bid
Bar code reader—CCD scanner	599	624	750	No bid	No bid
Printer—Laser	No bid	No bid	600	497	500
Printer—Receipt	N/A	695	897	No bid	No bid
Concentrator for LAN	No bid	No bid	No bid	234	135
Cabling	No bid	No bid	No bid	300	277
Uninterruptible power supply	300	355	No bid	233	277
Backup tape drive	No bid	No bid	366	305	228

Alternative specifications

This section on requesting bids is just an example. If you think you might want an alternative bid to include a client-server network, you should define the specifications for the file server. The specifications for a file server will probably include more Random Access Memory (RAM), a faster processor, and more hard disk storage. You may want a larger network. Just add more computers to the list, but be sure to increase the cabling specifications. It might be a good idea to request bids on some of the enhancements you may have already decided to add (see chapter 10). If the bids come in over budget, you can re-evaluate your automation project and design your final plan to fit your budget.

ELECTRICAL SUPPLY Bids for additional electrical work need to be part of your total project and part of your final proposal. Decide what you need to do and get two or three bids from licensed electrical contractors.

Plan for furniture

Decide what furniture you need and can afford, and get a few bids. It is better to include the cost for furniture you need in the cost of the project than to leave it out and hope you can find the money later. However, I would not hold up the entire project because you don't have enough money for furniture when you start the project.

In Great Bend we found that our regular library tables didn't work well as computer tables because of all the wires required for the computer hook-up. Many library furniture companies now make computer tables with enclosures for the wiring. This is not a part of your plan you can ignore. Over a period of a year we were able to purchase, at half price, three new computer tables that had been used once for display purposes at library and educational trade shows.

INSTALLATION AND TRAINING   Installation of the hardware and cabling should be included in the bid. You may wish to include installation of software, but it should be easy to install. If you elect to do it yourself to save money, make certain the contractor will provide a minimum amount of support over the telephone.

Training on the network should come from the provider. Hands-on experience seems to offer the best training for learning new software. On-screen help is also available in Windows.

MAINTENANCE AND SUPPORT   You will want to have a good idea of what your anticipated maintenance and support costs will be over the next five years, so that you can add those expenses to your ongoing operations budget. Maintenance and support should not be part of the start-up costs of the project. The cost of maintenance and support will likely have little effect on your final decision.

Summary

Soliciting bids is an important step in your automation project. You need to do it in a way that will keep your options open for as long as possible. Remember that the specifications in this chapter are only examples of current technology. New technology will be available by the time you are ready to request bids. You will want to get bids on the latest equipment you can afford. When we started planning for the Great Bend project, the 486 processor was the latest we thought we could afford. By the time we went out for bids, the cost of a Pentium computer was affordable for our file server.

Just remember that this chapter is more about the process of getting price information than it is about the specific pieces of hardware or software mentioned.

Suggested readings

Cibbarelli, Pamela R. "User Ratings of DOS and Windows IOLS Software." *Information Today*, (April 1995): 50-79.

Matthews, Joseph R. and Mark R. Parker, "Microcomputer-based Automated Library Systems: New Series, Part 1, 1993" *Library Technology Reports*, American Library Association, (March-April, 1993): 149-302.

Matthews, Joseph R. and Mark R. Parker, "Microcomputer-based Automated Library Systems: New Series, Part 2, 1993" *Library Technology Reports*, American Library Association, (March-April, 1993): 309-456.

In Great Bend we set up a computer with a bar code reader for the circulation staff while the data conversion was in progress. They gave themselves new borrower cards and checked out books to each other. By the time the circulation mode was up for the public the staff knew how to use it.

Developing the Final Plan

Chapter 7

You have gathered as much information as you can. You have looked at various automation systems and requested bids from vendors with the equipment and software you will need. You have received bids and know what various options will cost. You have carefully considered the options for data conversion, and how much they will cost. Now it is time to decide what you are really going to do and to commit it to a document you can submit to your board or administration for approval. It is time to put your plan in writing, and then to ask for the authorization to move ahead.

Considering cost

Unless you are one of a fortunate few, cost will always be on your mind. And while you will always be on the lookout for less expensive ways of doing things, you must also take the long view and think about what the final product will look like. The last thing you want to do is replace the bar codes on all the books or re-enter every bibliographic record on the automation system because of a bargain that didn't work out.

To develop the best plan for your library, you will have to continue to immerse yourself in the project. A large marker board placed in the office or staff room can help you and staff to stay on track. Write your automation goal at the top, and then use the board for ideas that come to you while working on the automation project or while doing other library tasks. You can come back to these ideas later and decide if they should be added to your automation plans.

Making the hard choices

Now that the time for gathering information is over, hard choices must be made. Indecision could delay the project. Wrong choices could cost valuable time or money, or both. Short-sighted decisions could prove costly in the future.

For many of the librarians I surveyed, getting the okay to implement the plan was not a problem. Their board or administration was behind them from the beginning. So for them it was a matter of deciding what they wanted to do, presenting the plan for final approval and then implementing it. For others the process was a little more difficult. The key to getting that final plan approved seemed to be involving the board, the staff and the administration in the process and keeping them informed all along the way.

> **Automate your collection right the first time, even if it costs a few dollars more.**

Here is a review and outline of some of the points we have covered. You can use this outline to help frame your final proposal.

- **Library Automation Software**   Decide which library automation package best meets the needs of your library. Think about your customers. Think about the staff. Think about the future—How happy will you be with your decision ten years from now? All other things being equal, price may be a deciding factor. The ideal match is when you really like one system better, and you can afford that system for the library.

- **Data Conversion**   Decide how you are going to load the bibliographic records on the system and link those records to the bar codes on the books. If you can afford it, a turnkey data conversion project is the way to go. Otherwise plan to spend a lot of your time, or somebody's time, completing the data conversion.

- **Computer Configuration**   Decide if you are going to use a stand-alone system, a peer-to-peer network or a client-server network. A peer-to-peer network with equally equipped workstations will work well for most small libraries.

- **Local Area Network and Cabling**   This will be part of the computer con-figuration decision. It is often wise to have a local contractor handle this part of the project.

- **Tape Backup and Uninterruptible Power Supply**   These are also part of the computer solution. Don't try to get by without them.

- **Bar Code Readers**   Decide which one to use and how many you will need. If the budget is limited, select the laser scanners, otherwise choose the CCD scanners. They are worth the money.

- **Printers**   Decide what you want to print, then decide what kind of print-ers you want and where to put them.

- **Electrical Access**   If you can, have a local contractor install a separate circuit for each computer.

- **Furniture**   Decide if the furniture you already own will be adequate or if you will have to purchase something new.

- **Installation and Training**   Determine who is going to do the training and who will be in charge of the day-to-day maintenance of the system.

- **Maintenance and Support**   Decide how hardware and software mainte-nance and support will be provided.

Reasons and costs

If you can discriminate between two or more options and reach a decision, you should have no trouble giving the reasons for your decision. In your final plan give the details that led to the decision you made. Your reasons could be as objective as "The computers from Company D cost less than the comput-ers from Company E." Or your reasons could be as subjective as "We didn't like the answers we got from the librarians we asked about Software Vendor B." Just call the shots the way you see them, and say, "This proposal repre-sents our best thinking after all the time we have spent trying to develop the best plan for our library."

Addressing community concerns

Your plan should address community concerns. Some people may be asking about the cost. Others may wonder why you haven't computerized the library before now. Others may worry that you are going to get rid of the card catalog. It is better to address the concerns straight on than to equivocate. Yes, automation costs a lot of money, but when it is up and running services will be improved and extended for everyone.

Tell patrons that you will keep the card catalog until it is not being used. Sooner or later they will find out that new books are only listed on the computer catalog.

There is no way I can possibly anticipate every objection you might hear from the community. The best thing I can tell you is to promote the automation system as a great advancement—a great tool for the staff and the public. Don't hide from the concerns of patrons. Most of them will support you if they feel you know what you are doing.

Getting the plan approved

By the time you get to this point, you should have a reasonably good idea of whether or not you can expect your plan to be approved. You may be in the enviable position of having a board that has supported the library's automation project from the beginning and approval of the plan is nothing more than a formality. In that case, you need to be very careful what you ask for, because you will probably get it. Several of the librarians I surveyed said that their boards or administrators had told them to automate. All they had to do was to figure out what to do and tell the board what they had decided.

On the other hand, if you have some reluctant board members who do not totally support the automation project, you may have to work a little harder to bring them along. It helps to involve them as much as possible from the beginning and ask for their opinions often.

Many board members cannot understand how automation will improve library service. The benefits are truly outside the scope of their experience. That is why it is so important to include board members on field trips to visit libraries that have automated.

In the end, you have to lay out the plan and ask the board to vote for it. After six months of developing the automation plan for the Great Bend Public Library, we still had some board members who were dragging their feet. After my final presentation to the Great Bend Board, one board member said, "Do we have to vote on this today?"

I replied, "No, we don't have to vote on this today, but postponing the vote won't change the plan. We have worked on this for six months. The staff is ready to go. They will be disappointed if we don't vote for it today. We have the money to do it, and I see no reason to postpone the vote." At that point I stopped talking and waited for them to make a motion and vote. They did and the vote was unanimous.

The critical point in this instance was that we had the money in the bank. More than likely that will be the case for you also. If you don't have the money in the bank, you may have to devise a way raise the funds for your automation project. With that possibility in mind, I have included a chapter on funding and fundraising. If you already have the money you can skip chapter 8.

Summary

Try to make as many decisions as you can with the help of others. In the end, however, when the staff is split on which automation system to buy, you will need to cast the deciding vote.

Don't let every decision be controlled by cost. Sometimes a better product with a better guarantee or a better reputation is worth more money. Some computers that are comparably equipped are not equal, and people in the business know which ones are better than others.

Be careful what you ask for because you might get it. Don't sell yourself or your library short. You are worth the best and so are the patrons of your library. Be positive. Be decisive. Go for what you want.

Suggested readings

Cohn, John M., Ann L. Klesey and Keith Michael Fiels. *Planning for Automation: A How-to-Do-It Manual for Librarians.* New York: Neal-Schuman, 1992.

Reynolds, Dennis. *Library Automation: Issues and Applications.* New York: R. R. Bowker, 1985.

Funding or Fundraising

Chapter 8

Finding the money to pay for automation may be a real concern to you at this point and, while it's not the principal focus of this book, here are a few ideas that may help you get the funding you need.

1. **Include your automation project in a building remodeling or expansion project.** This is precisely what many of the libraries we visited did. Their librarians used a need for a larger building to go for a bond election or a fundraising project and included the automation system with the equipment for their remodeled or new facility. It was part of the budget and the public accepted it. If you need a new building or need to renovate the one you have, why not include the money for automation in the total cost of your building project? It is easier to raise money for a new library and include automation than it is to raise money for automation alone.

2. **Fund your automation project from your regular budget over a period of a few years.** If you can afford one computer this year, buy it and begin your data conversion project. It may take you a year to get all of the book records converted. Buy the automation software the next year. Continue the data conversion, and buy more computers as you can afford them.

3. **Save for the automation project, and begin when you have enough money to start.** I don't recommend waiting too long. You could waste several years saving the money while the library could have been enjoying the blessings of automation.

4. **Try a lease with a five-year buy out.** Many banks and leasing companies offer public sector lease opportunities. For example, if you needed $15,000 for your automation project, you could lease the equipment for five years with a one-dollar buy out in five years at which time you would own the equipment. Your monthly payments would be about $350, or

For more ideas on fundraising, see *Fundraising for the Small Public Library* by James Swan (New York: Neal-Schuman, 1990).

The people in Chanute, Kansas, raised $2 million to renovate an old railroad station. Approximately $50,000 was needed to automate. By including this in the total price tag, the community accepted the automation project without thinking twice.

$4,200 per year. I don't recommend this option for every library because interest payments in the five years would be $5,700. It is always better to earn interest than to pay it. Leasing is an option worth considering if there are no other more viable ones.

5. **Ask the city to pay for your automation system out of their capital outlay budget.** If you are in a public library funded by the city, you can submit a proposal requesting capital funds from the city. You will be competing with other city agencies and may have to wait for your project to make it to the top of the city's priority list, but it is worth a try. This will give you the opportunity to weed your collection and do an inventory.

6. **If you are in a school library, ask for the money from the school district's capital fund.** Many school libraries have already automated, and many more are in the process of getting wired for automation and Internet access. Ask the superintendent to put the library's request for automation on the list of priorities. Some of the school librarians who answered my survey said that it was their principals who had proposed library automation.

7. **Write a request for federal funds.** State libraries administer funds from the federal government for library development. Many libraries have received grants from federal programs to help pay for their automation. Ask your state library for information on eligibility and application procedures.

8. **Write a grant proposal for a local foundation or corporation.** If you can demonstrate how a library automation project would benefit the workers of a local manufacturing plant, the parent corporation may be willing to fund the whole project. Local foundations that only fund local agencies are more likely to fund your project if you are in their geographic area of giving. Since there is a great deal of competition for national grants, you may be wiser to apply for local funding where the pool of applicants is smaller and strong local support for the library will help to promote your proposal.

9. **Raise funds through a capital campaign.** It may not be as easy as raising money for a new building, but it is worth a try. Develop a case statement that outlines what you want to do and the benefits of automating your library. Develop a chart of giving (see figure 8-1 on the next page). In this example, you will need a ten percent lead gift; two secondary gifts of five percent; five gifts of two percent; and ten gifts of one percent each. If you can raise that much money, you will be able to raise the rest in smaller gifts and other money-making activities.

A CHART OF GIVING is a fundraising technique often used in capital campaigns that divides the target amount into different segments. The fund-raiser uses these segments to target donors by the amount they can give. It is an effective technique because in successful campaigns, giving usually clusters around the target amounts.

CHART OF GIVING

Goal: $50,000

Size of Gift	Number	Amount	Percent	Individuals to Ask
Major Lead Gift	1	$5,000	10%	_____
				_____
				_____
Lead Gifts	2	$2,500	10%	_____
				_____
				_____
				_____
				_____
Major Gifts	5	$1,000	10%	_____
				_____
				_____
				_____
				_____
				_____
				_____
Big Gifts	10	$500	10%	_____
				_____
				_____
				_____
				_____
				_____
				_____
				_____
				_____
				_____

Figure 8-1: Chart of Giving

When it comes to fundraising remember that those persons in your community who use the library or who are familiar with its services will probably contribute to your project if you ask them. Those who are unfamiliar with the library will need more information or other incentives to contribute.

Brainstorming

If none of these ideas seem right for your library, why not try brainstorming? Sit down with a group of people who have the library's interest in common and think creatively. Brainstorming is a marvelous technique that can produce exciting, often unexpected results. You start with a group of seven to ten people who are somewhat familiar with the problem, but it is not necessary that everyone know everything about the operation of the library. Sometimes it is better if they don't. Set aside one hour of uninterrupted time. Assign two or more people to be note takers. Some brainstorming facilitators like to use newsprint sheets on an easel or big sheets taped to the wall. Select a leader to direct the discussion. Select someone else to do the writing. The facilitator encourages participation by making positive statements about the process. For example: "We are doing great. Let's keep it up. What else can we think of?" The leader reminds everyone of the rules, if that becomes necessary.

Rules for Brainstorming

1. Appoint a timekeeper and set a time limit. Twenty minutes is usually an optimum amount for the creative phase of brainstorming

2. Everyone contributes. You can start by going around the table. If a person can't think of anything the first time around, move on to the next person. Maybe he or she will have an idea the next time. Soon everyone will respond spontaneously.

3. All ideas are written down as they are given. The leader may repeat what has been said to give the contributor a chance to clarify the idea.

4. No evaluation of any kind is made at this time. Negative comments are especially discouraged. Even negative body language or laughing at an idea is discouraged.

Brainstorming works best when the group focuses on a specific question: "How can we find $50,000 for our automation project in the next six months." Write your focusing question on a blackboard or separate flip chart where everyone can see it.

Once people loosen up and get into the process, ideas will flow like water. I heard of a group of seven secretaries who came up with 256 ideas in one twenty-minute brainstorming session. It took five of them to write down all of the ideas. They weren't hampered by restraining thoughts of what wouldn't work, or if we do this, I will lose my job. Not all of the ideas were used, but think of the power this method has for creating solutions.

Facing the funding dilemma

In my work with the librarians and trustees in small public libraries, I have found that paying for automation is the biggest obstacle they face. More than likely your board faces similar concerns. Some members might wonder if automation is worth it. It is your job to show them in as many ways as you can how automation will benefit the patrons.

Trustees are struggling with the main responsibility of being a trustee—balancing their concern for adequate library service against the demands on the community to pay for it. In small libraries the struggle seems more intense. If it isn't the library board's job to make sure the library has the money it needs to meet the needs of the people, whose job is it? You may have to be the catalyst for change.

Who should ask?

Most experienced fundraisers believe that peers should make the actual solicitation, rather than the library director or staff. Many business and professional persons are asked for donations by individuals in the same economic bracket. They usually know one another, and they know where the money is located. They often owe favors to one another. The library director's role should be to provide background information or to answer any technical questions if they should arise.

Recruiting fund solicitors

Many board members and friends may volunteer for the responsibility of soliciting funds. If your library lacks a group large enough for the task, you might consider creating a special "citizen's advisory committee."

Ask your board and friends to list the most prominent persons in the community. Set up an appointment with them, preferably in small groups of six to twelve at a time. Explain that the board would like their opinion on an important step that would improve library service.

Prepare a concise description of the library's services and resources, as well as its governance, financing, usage, and needs. Summarize the advantages of automation and its costs. This is called a casebook, and it should be reviewed with each group by a board member or friend, with the library director present to answer questions. Discuss the chart of giving, and ask those present for their opinion about the feasibility of obtaining donations, the goal, and whether they agree with the levels of giving. Ask for their suggestions regarding potential donors. Depending on the tone of the discussion, see whether the group would be willing to help in soliciting funds. If there is any hesitancy, have a board member or friend call afterwards.It is quite likely that many will accept the responsibility. The library will increase the number of solicitors it has, and gain a good list of prospective donors.

The importance of asking

Fundraising is basically selling. It is selling a product or an idea or just a good feeling. It is selling an investment in your cause. The trick is packaging the product in a way that will make the other person want to buy.

Jim Keller is one of the best sales persons I know. He has been selling office products and equipment for at least 25 years. He says, "You have it in your mind that you are selling, but you want to relate to your prospects that they are not being sold something. You want to convey a feeling that you are working for them or with them to solve their problems. To do that you have to understand exactly what the customer has in mind."

Jim believes five essentials must be in place before someone will buy something. Whether you are going to buy a soda or a car, everyone of these has to be in place.

- **Is it the right product?**   If a farmer is looking for a pickup don't try to sell him a sports car.

- **Does the person need the product?**   If the person is thirsty, don't try to sell her a candy bar.

- **Is the price within the prospect's ability and willingness to pay?**

- **Is this the right time?**

- **Is it the right vendor?**   People do business with you because they like doing business with you.

Keller says, "When I'm not making progress, I stop and analyze where I am in the sales cycle. I try to determine where I am in relation to each of these five points. By asking questions, I try to find out which of the five I haven't met."

Everyone likes to be asked. It makes them feel important. You can do your best job of selling anything, but if you don't ask for it, you won't get the sale. In fundraising you have to ask for the gift.

Robert Hartsook, a professional fundraising consultant and a former fundraising executive for Wichita State University, said that most people give because they want to invest in what you are selling. They may believe that their contribution to the library's automation project is an investment in the future of the town, the lives of children, etc.

Getting to yes

What do you say when asking for a gift? Ask for a specific amount. Be direct. Ask for the money with strong verbs such as: give, donate or contribute. Don't say "We would appreciate it if you would consider making a generous donation." Your prospective donor can say "yes" to that question without giving a dime. He considered it and the answer is NO!

Here are a few ways to ask for a gift.

Please give…

Won't you please help?

The future of the library lies in your hands. You can make the difference. This is your chance to help…

With your help, we can go on. Help us reach our goal.

> **Remember to ASK FOR THE GIFT!** If you don't ask you won't get the money you need for your project.

FAVORITE FUNDRAISING TECHNIQUES

Here are a few of my favorite fundraising techniques that may help you with your automation project or some other need your library may have:

Used book sale.
Libraries are a natural for this one. For any other organization, I wouldn't recommend it. Make it big!

An auction.
One big push and then it is over. Makes a lot of money in a short time and everyone has a good time.

Door-to-door solicitation.
People respond when their friends and neighbors ask for donations.

Bake-less bake sale.
This will work well with library constituents. Tell them you need money for the library automation project. Then ask them if they would rather give you five dollars or make a cake and buy it back from the bake sale.

Be silent after the ask

This is one of the most critical pieces of advice on fundraising. After presenting your case say, "Will you help us with the automation project by giving $5,000." Don't say another word until the donor has spoken. Researchers have learned that the average silence in any conversation is less than three seconds. Learn to be comfortable with the silence. Let your prospective donor speak next. If your donor says "no," don't give up. Keep listening and talking. She may change her mind. If you don't get the gift, you shouldn't be disappointed. You have still learned something. You probably failed to predict the donor's capacity to give (how much discretionary cash she has) or her interest in the library.

Don't give up with the first visit. If you fail at the first try, try again or send someone else in a few days. Someone has said that it takes seven askings to get to yes. Your donor may change her mind after thinking about your request.

Summary

Finding the money to automate a small library may not be a big problem for some librarians, but judging from the small libraries I have seen, it is often the biggest problem. Their libraries would have automated if they had the funds.

Finding money for needed library projects is a constant challenge. While fundraising is not a major part of automating a library, overcoming the financial obstacles is important. Librarians, board members and administrators need ideas to help them see beyond the cost of automation.

Suggested readings

Burlingame, Dwight, ed. *Library Fundraising: Models for Success,* Chicago: American Library Association, 1995.

Burger, Janette M. compiler. *Grant Funding: How Everyone Benefits,* McHenry, Illinois: Follett Software Company, 1993.

Hall, Mary. *Getting Funded: A Complete Guide to Proposal Writing.* 3rd ed. Portland: Continuing Education Publications, Portland State University, 1988.

Swan, James, *Fundraising for the Small Public Library: A How-to-Do-It Manual for Librarians.* New York: Neal-Schuman, 1990.

Winning the Money Game. New York: Baker and Taylor, 1979.

You're in the Money! Fundraising Fundamentals. (videocassette) Towson, Maryland: American Library Association Video/Library Video Network, 1994.

Implementation

Chapter 9

After your plan is approved you will order and install the various components of the automation project and begin data conversion. I suggest you develop a timeline for implementation similar to the one in appendix D. The timeline will help you focus on the activities you need to accomplish and on the order in which they need to be done. Having a timeline helped us stay on target; however, we grossly underestimated how much time it would take for data conversion. The list of tasks to be completed outlines the implementation process.

Getting organized

If you have more than a few staff members, you may want to appoint teams and assign various tasks to each. It is important to involve support staff as well as department heads in the teams. Everyone needs a sense of ownership. Your teams may look a little different, but this list and the charges assigned to each team will give you some ideas to get you started:

Bar Code and Borrower Card Team You will have to make some decisions about bar codes. Recommendations will be needed for patron number range, materials number range, and temporary number range. Later on you will design the borrower cards.

Job Descriptions Team The nature of the work you do and the way you do it will change for everyone. You will have to look at every job description and make the necessary changes. These will change during the data conversion process and afterwards. Everyone will need to be flexible, be willing to assume new duties, and to give up old ones.

Data Conversion Team You have a tremendous task ahead of you, and we are not sure how long it will take. Everyone will be expected to help with placing bar codes on the books and editing the bibliographic records in the database. You will need to make decisions about the MARC records and how to display call numbers and local holdings.

Circulation Policy Team   The automation system will allow you to do things that could never have been done before. You will need to make recommendations to the board about overdue fines, limits on the number of books checked out, and holds—plus develop a list of other circulation issues for consideration.

Public Awareness and Instruction Team   You will want to involve the community in the project. You will have the task of developing materials for patron instruction, planning for ceremonies, and making public announcements. You will need to have a few public meetings to introduce the system to the community. This committee will make recommendations regarding promotional ideas such as naming the computer, auctioning the first card, or using gold cards to denote special privileges.

CD-ROM Software Selection Team   Each workstation may come with a built-in CD. This will give you the opportunity to try many products on CD. The CD team will seek input, evaluate and make recommendations for the purchase of CDs.

Computer Deployment Team   This team will make recommendations about the configuration and deployment of computer workstations. The team will also make recommendations about which computers will have access to which services.

Patron Registration and Profile Team   This team will make recommendations about patron registration process and information. You need to look at the state statistical report to gather the information you need to complete the report. You will need to determine the staffing requirement and timeline for re-registering borrowers.

The teams in Great Bend did their work without administrative interference. There was some initial concern about the work of the Job Description Team. Some staff members were afraid that their job assignments would be changed without their input. That was never part of the plan. One good way to lose the support of the staff for the automation project is to tell the board that you will be able to reduce staff once automation is in place. A person who spends most of his or her day filing circulation cards could feel threatened by such a promise.

> **The implementation phase is the time to reassure and continue to continually reassure staff members about their work and their jobs.**

Some policies may need to be updated

The automation project may require the library to change some of its policies. We had to change our overdue policy because the automation system based its fine calculation on a daily fine. Before automation our fines were based on the cost of generating the notice. Our reserve policy changed because the computer could place a hold automatically and a staff member didn't have to spend time looking through the check-out file to place a hold.

The work of data conversion

If you plan to send the shelflist out for data conversion and use smart bar codes, the process will be a little different from in-house data conversion and the use of dumb bar codes.

Data conversion using smart bar codes

The database is load onto the computer and the smart bar codes are placed on the books. You can save staff time by using volunteers to help with putting the bar codes on books. Once this process is completed, you are ready to start checking out books. Implementation is simple, but you may spend months, even years, cleaning up your database.

Data conversion using a CD-ROM utility

If you plan to use a CD-ROM utility to locate your MARC records, you will have to install the CD-ROM drives and the CD software. Then you can start your data conversion project. If you are working on a shoestring, you don't even have to buy the automation software before you start the data conversion. You can attach dumb bar codes to the books, do a search for the MARC records and save the selected records on floppy disks.

I suggest you find an area away from regular library activities that can be designated for the data conversion project. Many of the library work areas I have seen tend to become cluttered. You may need a space where you can concentrate on the job and not be interrupted by other concerns. You may need a space where work can be left undisturbed in the event of an interruption. In Great Bend we closed the art room and used it for our data conversion—one of the best decisions we made.

To get started, select a tray of shelflist cards and the corresponding books to the designated work area. Follow the instructions you get with the CD-ROM product. You will look up records on the CD by International Standard Book Number (ISBN) or some other unique marker connected with the record. When you find the record, it will be downloaded onto a floppy disk or the hard drive. You can modify the record—add or delete subject headings, add your call number, or change other bits of information. If you haven't purchased the software yet, the records will be saved and then imported into the automated system after you buy the software.

If you want to use smart bar codes, you can send a copy of your bibliographic records to a company that produces them, or they can be produced in-house with the appropriate software and equipment.

You may also want to send the database out for authority control work after completing the data conversion. While you can count on consistency of records from the CD-ROM utility, authority control is not guaranteed. If your collection is small and you are willing to accept the level of authority control provided by the CD-ROM utility, simply proceed past this step.

If you have chosen to use dumb bar codes, you will probably want to load the books on a cart and take them to the data conversion area. Bar code labels will be placed on the books, and bar code numbers will be linked to the record in the database before materials are returned to the shelves.

If you have purchased your automation software and your subscription to the CD-ROM utility, and you are going to use dumb bar codes you can follow this procedure:

1. Load books from the stacks on to a book truck.

2. Take the books to the data conversion area.

3. Look up the records on the CD-ROM utility for each book on the cart.

4. Download the records to a file.

5. Attach the bar code labels to the books.

6. Link the bar code number on the book to the data record on the computer.

7. Check the record and edit it to reflect the bibliographic information in the book.

8. Return the books to the shelves, and take the next batch of books to the data conversion area.

Data conversion worksheet

No matter which method you decide to use, you will have to develop a standardized process for adding titles to the database. Then you will create a document that details step-by-step instructions for those who will do the data conversion. Even if you are the only one who will be doing the work, you need a procedural document to help you do the same process the same way every time.

The sample data conversion worksheet on the next page (see figure 9.1) was created by Kathy Mitchum, Reference and Acquisitions Department Head for the Great Bend Public Library. It was designed to ensure that everyone on the team was performing data conversion consistently. Your instructions will be different, depending on the system you select. The worksheet that follows is one example that may be helpful in developing your own worksheet.

Completing the data conversion

Completing the data conversion phase of your project is sort of like eating an elephant. You do it one bite at a time. It goes faster if one person can use two computers at the same time. It takes the computer a minute or more to index and save each record. While you are saving a record on one computer, you could be using the second computer to link the bar code to the book and edit the record. By the time you are ready to save the record on the second computer, the first computer will be ready for another record.

Re-registration of borrowers

By the time you get to this point, you will have a good idea where you are going with the rest of the project. You have weeded your collection and completed an inventory. You have selected and purchased your hardware and software, and connected it all together in a network. Your data conversion is moving along nicely, and you are planning for the day you will start checking out books. However, I wouldn't recommend that until all of your circulating collection is linked to a data record.

DATA CONVERSION WORKSHEET

1. Clean the book corner (Back, upper right) with alcohol. When dry, affix the bar code label with the numerals running along the spine (1/2 inch from each corner).

2. At WELCOME TO ATHENA, click on CATALOGING (at the bottom of the screen).

3. Select CHANGE COLLECTION PARAMETERS. Click on CHANGE COLLECTION. Search for the appropriate collection and select it. Click on GO BACK and click on arrow for MAINTAIN TITLES COPIES.

4. Type word or phrase to search. Press Enter to search. On "Search Results" screen, click on the appropriate title.

5. Click on TITLES/COPIES (right side of screen). This will bring up the MARC record.

6. Use the cursor to arrow down through the record. Spot check it all, but pay special attention to the following MARC tags for necessary information and check with the shelflist and/or book:

    100 Author's name

    245 Title

    600s Subjects

    Check if there is a 655 =2 field that says: "gsafd" or other nonsense looking data. Delete these.

    If a word has diacritics of any sort, the display may need correcting.

    For JUV books, there may be both a "650 0" field and a "650 1" field. If they are identical (except for the subheadings of "juvenile literature"), keep only the one that contains the subheading "juvenile literature." Delete the other tag(s).

7. Finally, check the 852 tag. This is the local holding field. To correct this information (if necessary), go to COPIES.

    a) Scan the bar code. If there is something in this field (i.e. temporary identification number assigned by Athena® or Auto-Graphics®), delete it first. One easy way is to double click on the temporary number (which will highlight the number) and then scan in the new bar code number.

    b) CALL PREFIX: Type one of the following: J, REF, Auto Ref, Consumer Center, Picture Book, etc.

    c) CALL MAIN: Type the Dewey number, B, or FIC.

    d) CALL SUFFIX: Type v., year, [v. 1- or v.2 or 1980 or 1980-82, etc.]

    e) FORMAT: Use the following abbreviations exactly:

    hb=hard back

    pb=paperback

    video =video

    audio=audio cassette

    f) COST: Type the actual cost from the book or the card. For those books that a cost cannot be found, leave blank. DO NOT use a dollar sign.

    g) DATE ACQ.: Type the date, e.g. 9-94.

    h) NOTE: Type a note if the book card has a designation about the books inclusion in Fiction Catalog, Public Library Catalog, Children's Catalog, Handicraft Index, Short Story Index, etc.

8. When finished with a record, click on SAVE.

9. The program returns you to the search screen. Scan the bar code on the book to verify that the entry was completed.

10. You are ready for the next book. Repeat this process for every book."

Figure 9.1: Data Conversion Worksheet.

Before you can check out books to the patrons using the system, you will have to get their names into the computer. If you are in a school and the school has automated enrollment records, you may be able to download patron information from their files into your library automation system. If you are in a public library you will probably have to put the names in one key stroke at a time. This is not a lot of fun, so I suggest you start doing it several weeks before you plan to start checking out books.

You could take your current borrower files and type them into the computer, but I don't recommend it. Your patron records are likely to be very inaccurate. People have moved, married, changed their names, gotten a different telephone number, or even died. You don't want to put inaccurate information in the computer.

I recommend that you re-register everyone. You need to develop a form that will give you all the information you need. Review the computer screens for patron information (see figure 9.2) and then create a form you will ask your patrons to complete (see figure 9.3). Be certain to arrange the information fields on the patron form so they are parallel to the related fields on the computer screen. A staff member who has ten people lined up to get a new card doesn't need to look all over the page to find the next bit of information the computer requires. If the forms are not parallel, hurried staff members typing the information into the computer will be more prone to making mistakes. If the volume of patrons waiting to register becomes overwhelming, have staff enter their names, scan the new card number, and give them their cards. The patron information on the computer can be updated later when the rush is over.

New borrower cards

As you re-register your borrowers, you need to give them a new borrower number that is the same as their bar code. You can give them a new card with a bar code, or you can get a bar code label and put it on their old card. I vote for the first choice because a new card signals the beginning of a new way to check out books. You are leaving the old behind, including their old card, and starting fresh with a new card and a new system.

New cards will cost between twenty and thirty cents each. Bar code labels for old cards will cost about five cents each. If cost is a concern, you may choose not to give patrons cards at all. You can simply add their names to the borrower database and search by their names on the computer each time they check out a book.

Giving out new cards and re-registering your borrowers will give you the opportunity to do several things that will help the library:

1. You can purge your patron files of all inactive borrowers who have moved away or those who have died.

2. You can update your files by getting current information on all library patrons.

3. You could conduct a user survey by asking those who re-register questions about their use of the library and which library services they prefer.

Invite individuals to the library to get a new library card. Invite families to come together. This is especially helpful if your policy requires that parents sign for their children. It will cut down on confusion, and it will be a fun family activity. The event can also be an opportunity to promote your services or teach patrons about the

Patron Registration Screens

First Screen

Patron ID

Alternate ID

Surname

First Name

Group 1

Group 2

Group 3

Address Screen

Patron ID

Surname

Address

City

State   Phone Number

ZIP

Alternate Screen

Patron ID

Surname

Address

City

State   Phone Number

ZIP

Other Screen

1

2

3

4

5

6

7

8

Library Card Application

(Identification Required)

Bar Code Number (Library Use Only)   Verified ID (Social Security # or Driver's License#, etc.)

Last Name   First Name   Middle

Are you over 18?   Are you home bound?   Are you a Staff/Board member?
Yes   No   Yes   No

Are a city resident?   Which county do you live in?
Yes   No

Birthday (Month/Day)   Are you a student?   If so, which school?
                         Yes   No

Mailing Address   Apt. or Space Number

City

State   Telephone

ZIP   Alternate Telephone

Place of Employment

Address of Employer   Telephone

City   State   ZIP

Name of parent or spouse

Name of family member or friend not living with you

Address   City   State   ZIP

Telephone

Are you a temporary resident?   If so, until when?
Yes   No

Permanent Address   City   State   ZIP

(Figure 9-2)

Figure 9.2: Patron Registration Screens.   **Figure 9.3: Library Card Application.**

4. Because of automation you will be able to secure, record, and recover information about your patrons that you could not access before. For example, whether or not the person lives outside the city limits may be valuable information required for a report.

    The only reason you register patrons is to recover the material they borrow from the library. If they need a reminder or if they move before they return their books, you need to know how to reach them. Do not ask for information you don't need.

Patron orientation

You can use the re-registration process as a time to instruct patrons on the use of the new system. You could create a ten- to fifteen-minute video on the automation system and show it while library users are waiting to get their new card. The video can be used to demonstrate a simple search or two. You can also show a more complex search, but don't attempt too much in this brief introduction—maybe something like looking for a video on breadmaking. The video should also include the new check out procedure or any changes in date due notices. This would be a good time to review circulation policies and give a brief update on some of the library's services—new and old.

Surveying your patrons

"Our job is to give the people what they want when they come to the library." This is our motto at the Great Bend Public Library. We can't keep that promise if we don't ask our customers what they want. So we often ask, "Did you get what you wanted at the library today?" When we ask our regular patrons, they will likely answer that they are getting exactly what they want; don't change a thing. However, by surveying everyone who comes in for a new library card you may reach some of the people on the fringes—those who don't use the library quite as often. You may learn more from them than from your regular customers.

Here is a sample survey you can redesign to meet your needs.

Library User Survey

1. How often do you use the library?
   __ Weekly or more often.
   __ Several times a month.
   __ Once a month or less.
   __ Once a year or less.

2. Do you usually get what you want when you come to the library?
   __ Yes, almost always.
   __ Yes, most of the time.
   __ Sometimes.
   __ Not very often.

3. If you didn't get what you wanted, what could we do in the future to make sure you get what you wanted when you come to the library?
   _____

4. When you come to the library, what services do you use most often? (You may check more than one.)
   __ Check out fiction books to read.
   __ Find information for a job- or business-related interest.
   __ Find information related to home, personal interest, or hobby.
   __ Find information on a health related issue.
   __ Bring a child to story hour.
   __ Read the newspapers or magazines.
   __ Get tax forms and information.
   __ Attend a Brown Bag Book Review or some other program.
   __ Work on my family history research.
   __ Other use. _____

5. What kinds of books do you like to read?
   _____

6. What research materials are most helpful to you?
   _____

7. Which library services do you use the most?
   _____

8. If the library had the resources, what additional services what would you like?
   _____

Figure 9.4: Library User Survey.

Training staff members

This is an individual issue. Some library staff members may require more scheduled training; others may require very little. Windows applications with on-screen help may be sufficient for those who are computer literate already. In Great Bend, we set up several computers in various staff areas to let staff members become acquainted with the software without the stress of being in front of the public. They issued library cards to themselves and checked out books for themselves and other staff members. There was no administrative directive to learn the system. Out of a sense of commitment to the job and a desire to learn the new system, the staff began using the new system with few or no formal training sessions. This doesn't mean that formal training isn't important. If you think you need it, spend the money and hire someone from the automation software company to provide hands-on training.

Don't expect too much from training

Don't count on training to overcome the reluctance to learn the system. That reluctance may be the result of fear of losing a job. Formal training will help if the staff needs a little help learning. It won't help if they don't want to learn.

Educating the patrons

Children will take to the automation system like ducks to water. They are fearless and think they know all about your computer system. They will sit at a computer and start punching keys without knowing what they are doing or even trying to do. Everyone else may need some help. Older patrons will read everything on the screen before they make a move. Others may need a little coaching. They may try to use the system without reading the screen carefully, and then not get what they want.

You may want to set up an information desk in the public area to help people become acquainted with the system. It is best to let the patrons get their hands on the computer rather than doing their for them. They will learn how to use the system with experience. If you do searches for them, they will only learn to let you do the same thing the next time.

Another good idea is a little, one-page folder explaining how to use the system. You can hand these out when you re-register patrons. As much as possible try to make your handout look like the computer screen. Make the print large with lots of white space. Keep it simple. Don't try to cram the whole technical manual on one page—no one will read it if you do.

Inaugurating the system

Once you get all the books on the computer, and the patrons have had a chance to get new library cards; you are ready to open the system to the public. There are two trends of thought on this event. Doing it quietly will make it easier on the staff. They will be able to serve the public at their usual pace, and they will be better able to deal with unforeseen problems. The other approach is to have a grand opening of the library's automation system, including a big splash in the newspaper and on television and radio. This will create lots of visibility for the library and more work for the staff. You and your staff need to decide what is best for your library.

The last thing you do before closing down your manual system is to transfer all information on currently circulating materials. If you don't, all of the books on your database will come up on the computer as "IN" when in fact some of them are checked out. You may choose to close the library for a day or two to get all the circulation computers installed and the OPAC terminals in place.

Date due notification

Another implementation issue is how you will let the patrons know when their books are due. You could continue to stamp the date due on the slip inside the book, but that seems to defeat one of the purposes of automating. You may want to stamp a card with the date due and put it in the book. Some libraries have used adhesive price tag machines and then at some point they remove the stickers. Some systems will support receipt or slip printers. Other systems allow you to print the screen after the transaction is complete. Check with other librarians to see what they have done, but most of the librarians I have talked with seem less than satisfied with the system they are currently using. They are still looking for a better way.

Celebrate your success

After you have the system up and everything is running the way you want it to, have a party for the staff and the board. Congratulate yourself. Bask in your success. Figure out a way to recognize every staff member. Everyone deserves a pat on the back. If you have someone clever on the staff, try some funny recognition certificates, like the "sticky finger award" for the person who put the most bar code labels on the books. Most of all, have fun!

Summary

Implementation can be the fun part of your automation project. It can also be the longest and most boring. No matter what you decide to do, data conversion will take a lot more time than you think. You need to celebrate intermediate accomplishments. When the Great Bend staff finished the data conversion for all the adult fiction, we all went out for breakfast instead of having a staff meeting. We kept a tote board in the data conversion room to keep track of the number of shelves we had completed.

Implementation never quite goes one hundred percent as planned. That is why is it always important to keep your options open. When you finish, your automated library will be the best thing your patrons have ever seen. They will love it and so will the staff.

Suggested readings

Corbin, John. *Implementing the Automated Library System.* Phoenix: Oryx Press, 1988.

Tracy, Joan I. *Library Automation for Library Technicians.* Metuchen, New Jersey: Scarecrow Press, 1986.

Enhancements

Chapter 10

Once you have your automation system up and running, you will want to consider what you can add to make it more valuable to your patrons and the staff. You may have already decided to include enhancements with your basic automation plan. That is fine.

If it appears that it could take some time to have your system completely operating, you may want to wait until you have the system ready for the public until you buy some of the enhancements. Technology is changing so fast that state-of-the-art equipment you buy this year may have been replaced in six months; or it may be available for a fraction of what you have paid for it. Buy the newest technology you can afford, but avoid buying equipment that may become obsolete before you can get adequate use from it.

Here are a few enhancements you may want to consider:

More Computers My first recommendation as an enhancement to your automation system is more computers. Unless your library is very small you will probably need more than three computers. You could either attach other equipment to this computer for other services or connect it to the automation system to search the catalog. You may need more computers for staff use. If your children's department is separated from the adult department, you may want a computer in each department.

Fax Modem A fax modem is relatively inexpensive and can enhance the library's ability to give patrons what they want at the library. The fax modem turns your printer into a fax machine, with the capability to send faxes from your computer and to receive faxes from any other fax machine. You could receive copies of magazine articles from another library in a matter of minutes.

Printers Attaching a printer to the public access computers will be a much-appreciated enhancement. If you are operating under Windows, you need to have a laser printer or an ink-jet printer because they can handle the graphics found in Windows applications.

> **MODEM** stands for Modulator-Demodulator. It is a device that changes digital signals of a computer to analog signals to enable two or more computers to communicate with each other over conventional telephone lines via dial access.

CD-ROM Drive or Tower   You can buy a CD tower that will hold multiple CDs. Lots of very sophisticated reference tools are now available on CD. Some of them are rather expensive for a small library, but you will want to take a good look and decide if your budget can stand it. A license to use them on a network will cost more than a license for a stand-alone unit. I would recommend attaching a CD-ROM tower to one of the public access computers on the network. This would give the public access to the local online catalog and all of the CDs you load on the CD drives.

Internet   If you want to provide a great service, give the public access to the Internet. The Internet has all kinds of information—some good and some not so good, but you will have to sort through those issues. If you plan to offer Internet service to your customers, you need a computer dedicated to that application. You will have to develop policies to ensure equitable access. You may have to put time limits on use of this machine and offer scheduling to ensure access for as many users as possible.

You will need a high speed modem and another telephone line unless you want to let the public tie up your library line surfing the Internet. Finding an Internet provider that will sell you unlimited service for a fixed fee is critical to containing your costs. You cannot have someone connected to the Internet with the clock ticking, and the library paying for whatever time is charged.

The Internet will also give you access to e-mail, which can be used for interlibrary loan or for information requests to other libraries. Most libraries do not allow patrons to establish personal mail boxes for e-mail. However, e-mail is an increasingly popular way to communicate in organizations of all sizes.

> **Here is a short list of CD products worth considering.**
> Encyclopedias
> Dictionaries
> Telephone directories
> Street atlases
> Family history research tools
> Book selection tools
> Periodical indexes
> Health & medical resources
> Poetry indexes
> Legal reference tools

> **E-MAIL** stands for electronic mail. E-mail is a method used to electronically exchange messages (mail) between individuals who are connected to a network.

Developing a contingency fund

No matter how hard you try to control costs, your automation system will cost more than you think. Even if computer costs go down and other costs remain about the same, you will most assuredly find something else you need for the automation system. Software maintenance will cost about ten percent of the purchase price every year you use the software. Some of the hardware pieces will need to be repaired or replaced within three years. These are all good reasons to develop a contingency fund. I recommend a contingency of at least ten percent of your total automation cost. More than that wouldn't hurt.

Realistically, you should begin developing an equipment replacement fund when you get the system up and running, because it will probably need to be replaced in five to seven years. We have been buying and using microcomputers since 1981. Most of the computers we bought more than five years ago still work fine, but they are no longer able to handle the applications we use. It would be a good idea to set aside twenty percent the hardware costs each year. If the hardware for your automation cost $10,000, you need to set aside $2,000 each year for equipment replacement. You will be glad you did.

Continue to work with software vendor

As I mentioned earlier, signing up with a library automation software company is like entering into a marriage. Working together will be beneficial for both of you, but a divorce will be very painful. Start by contracting for software maintenance. Like partners in a marriage you have to communicate in order to get what you want from the relationship. Tell them what you want. Then join their users' group and work with other librarians to secure the enhancements you want in the software. Other librarians are probably looking for similar improvements.

Summary

Enhancements are what you add to the automation system after the basic system is in place, and you still have some money to add a bell or a whistle. If you have the money, you could include some or all of these enhancements in your original plan and look for others.

Technology is moving so fast that librarians will have to run just to keep up; even then, they may not be able to enjoy every new piece of available technology.

Suggested readings

Bock, Wally. *Getting on the Information Superhighway.* Menlo Park, California: Crisp Publications, 1996.

Engle, Mary E., and others. *Internet Connections: A Librarian's Guide to Dial-Up Access and Use,* (LITA Monograph 3). Chicago: Library and Information Technology Association, 1993.

Machovec, George. *Telecommunications, Networking, and Internet Glossary.* Chicago: Library and Information Technology Association, 1993.

Negroponte, Nicholas P. *Being Digital.* New York: Alfred A. Knopf, 1995.

Evaluation

Chapter 11

After the system has been in operation for about six months, it is time to evaluate your progress. Sit down with the staff in a meeting and ask, "What could we have done differently?" "What can we do now to make automation work better for our patrons and ourselves?"

Then do the same with the library board. You're sure to learn some things that will help you to improve service to patrons.

Bring out some of your original assumptions and ask the hard questions.

- Has automation increased access to information through improved indexing of the existing collection? If the answer is "yes," how can we measure the increase?

- Have research techniques been enhanced through automation's access to sophisticated tools, such as CD-ROM products and online databases? How can we measure our success?

- Are patrons using the automation system's ability to tell them if a book is checked out or not?

- Does the reference staff have quicker and more complete access to the entire collection? How can we measure our success?

- Are our patrons able to access the library's collection from their homes? How many times a week do they dial in?

- Can the circulation staff create accurate lists of materials patrons have checked out? How many lists are we creating a week?

- Are we placing reserves on books automatically? How many are we placing a week?

- Are we verifying patron information automatically with every transaction? Is this helping us catch delinquent borrowers?

- Can we tell patrons when a book that is checked out is expected to be returned? How often do we do this?

- Does the automated circulation system check books in and out faster? Has this resulted in an increase in circulation?

- Does the system generate overdue notices automatically? Is this function working well?

- Are more books coming back on time?

- Have patrons learned how to search the collection by format, i.e. videos.

- Have we simplified borrower registration?

- Have we sped up the inventory process?

- Have we eliminated the filing of all cards? If not, which ones do we still file?

- How much time are we saving on maintaining the public catalog?

- Do we provide the opportunity for public access to the Internet? How many people access it every week?

- Have there been any unexpected benefits from the automation project? What were they? How can we measure them?

How much did the project really cost?

You may not want to know the answer to this question, but it is still worth asking. The answer will probably be, "More than we ever planned for." The board and the administration will want to know. You should want to know. So get out the invoice file and figure it out sometime. Just make sure that you present the answer in the context of the benefits the library has enjoyed.

Promote the success of automation

The library's automation system represents a major commitment of time and library resources. There is no reason for it not to be a success. Take every opportunity to tell people about it. You could use the success of your automation project to spotlight the library in the newspaper, on the radio or television. Write a brief description of the automation project and publish it for your patrons. Use the report to highlight some of the features of the system and explain how patrons can take advantage of them.

Summary

Evaluating your success will help you feel good after a long difficult task. It will help you feel that the effort was worth it.

You will also learn ways you can improve the capabilities of the automation system. You could learn that some of the benefits you were supposed to derive from automating are not happening because you haven't been promoting them.

Automation is within your reach. If you can write down a goal to automate your library and then work to make it happen, it will happen and you will be happy for the journey.

Weeding Flow Chart

Appendix A

To simplify the process of weeding, I have created a flow chart. If you familiarize yourself with the tools in chapter 2 you will be able to use this chart to weed all of the book collections in your library. The squares arranged like baseball diamonds call for you to make a decision. Follow the path for each book and you will be able to get through your collection quickly.

---

*Unacceptable appearance includes:

Pages are yellowed, mutilated or torn.

Print is small or unreadable.

Cover is tattered, dull, or dingy.

**Unacceptable reasons to keep a book:

Someone may want to read this book sometime.

This book is bound to be a classic someday.

Mayor Jones gave us this book 25 years ago.

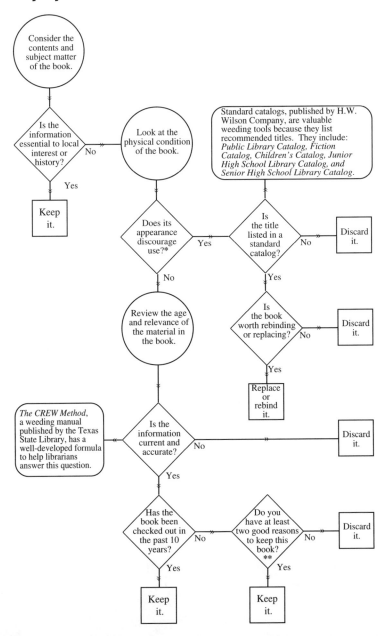

Consider the contents and subject matter of the book.

Is the information essential to local interest or history? — No

Yes → Keep it.

Look at the physical condition of the book.

Standard catalogs, published by H.W. Wilson Company, are valuable weeding tools because they list recommended titles. They include: *Public Library Catalog, Fiction Catalog, Children's Catalog, Junior High School Library Catalog, and Senior High School Library Catalog.*

Does its appearance discourage use?* — Yes → Is the title listed in a standard catalog? — No → Discard it.

No ↓ | Yes ↓

Review the age and relevance of the material in the book.

Is the book worth rebinding or replacing? — No → Discard it.

Yes ↓

Replace or rebind it.

The CREW Method, a weeding manual published by the Texas State Library, has a well-developed formula to help librarians answer this question.

Is the information current and accurate? — No → Discard it.

Yes ↓

Has the book been checked out in the past 10 years? — No → Do you have at least two good reasons to keep this book?** — No → Discard it.

Yes ↓ | Yes ↓

Keep it. | Keep it.

Appendix B

Inclusion of a vendor on this list does not constitute endorsement of any kind. Neither does the exclusion of vendors constitute non-endorsement. Additional vendors can be identified by visiting conference exhibits and by keeping current with the professional literature. State librarians and cooperative systems may also be able to suggest other firms.

Automation Software Vendors

Annie Library Automation
4600 S. Ulster Street #260
Denver, Colorado 80237
303/740-9300

Athena Automation System
NICHOLS Advanced Technologies
3452 Losey Boulevard South
La Crosse, Wisconsin 54601
608/787-8333

BiblioFile
The Library Corporation
Research Park
Inwood, West Virginia 25428-9733
304/229-0100

CALICO Company
P. O. Box 6190
Chesterfield, Missouri 63006-6190
800/367-0416

CASPR, Inc.
635 Vaqueros Avenue
Sunnyvale, California 94086
408/522-9800

Cordant, Inc.
11400 Commerce Park Drive
Reston, Virginia 22091-1506
703/758-7000

Data Trek Inc.
5838 Edison Place
Carlsbad, California 92008
619/431-8400

Eloquent Systems Inc.
25-1501 Lonsdale Avenue
Vancouver, British Columbia
V7M 2J2
604/980-8358

IMPACT/SLiMS System
Auto-Graphics, Inc.
3201 Temple Avenue
Pomona, California 91768
800/776-6939

MAXCESS Library Systems, Inc.
4126 Warner St.
Kensington, Maryland 20895
301/564-1350

McGraw-Hill School Systems
20 Ryan Ranch Road
Monterey, California 93940
800/663-0544

New Generations Technologies
Dept. 844
P. O. Box 34069
Seattle, Washington 98124
800/661-7112

On Point, Inc./TLC Total
Library Computerization
2606 36th NW
Washington, DC 20007-1419
202/338-8914

Precision One Integrated System
Brodart Automation
500 Arch Street
Williamsport, Pennsylvania 17705
717/326-2461

Sirsi Corporation
689 Discovery Drive
Huntsville, Alabama 35806
205/922-9825

SIRS Mandarin Library
Automation System
SIRS Incorporated
P.O. Box 2348
Boca Raton, Florida 33427-2348
561/994-0079

Unison Automation System
Follett Software Company
1391 Corporate Drive
McHenry, Illinois 60050-7401
815/344-8700

**Western Research and
Development Limited**
8113 Hynds Blvd.
Cheynne, Wyoming 82009-1606
307/632-5656

Winnebago Automation System
Winnebago Software Company
P.O. Box 430
Caledonia, Minnesota 55921
507/724-5411

When you contact automation software vendors, ask them for product information, pricing, and names and addresses of some of their clients.

Data Conversion Vendors

BiblioTECH Corporation
61 Hickory Road
Sudbury, Massachusetts 01776
508/443-9167

Brodart Automation
500 Arch Street
Williamsport, Pennsylvania 17705
717/326-2461

Catalog Card Company
12221 Wood Lake Drive
Burnsville, Minnesota 55337
612/882-8558

Follett Software Company
1391 Corporate Drive
McHenry, Illinois 60050-7401
815/344-8700

Gaylord Information Systems
Box 4901
Syracuse, New York 13221-4901
800/272-3414

MARCHIVE, Inc.
P. O. Box 47508
San Antonio, Texas 78265
210/646-6161

Nichols Advanced Technologies
3452 Losey Boulevard South
La Crosse, Wisconsin 54601
608/787-8333

OCLC Inc.
National Sales Division
6565 Frantz Road
Dublin, Ohio 43017-3395
800/848-5878

Retro Link Associates, Inc.
A Division of Ameritech Library Services
175 N. Freedom Blvd. Suite 108
Provo, Utah 84601
801/375-6508

Sirsi Corporation
689 Discovery Drive
Huntsville, Alabama 35806
205/922-9825

Winnebago Software Company
P.O. Box 430
Caledonia, Minnesota 55921
507/724-5411

CD-ROM Bibliographic Utilities

Alliance Plus
Follett Software Company
1391 Corporate Drive
McHenry, Illinois 60050-7401
815/344-8700

BiblioFile
The Library Corporation
Research Park
Inwood, West Virginia 25428-9733
304/229-0100

Precision One
Brodart Automation
500 Arch Street
Williamsport, Pennsylvania 17705
800/233-8467 ext. 784

Library of Congress
Cataloging Distribution Service
Customer Services Section
Washington, DC 20541-5017
202/707-6100

SWL, Inc.
Multi-Media Products Division
5383 Hollister Ave.
Santa Barbara, California 93111
805/964-7724

Providers of Authority Control

Blackwell North America, Inc.
6024 SW Jean Road, Building G
Lake Oswego, Oregon 97035
503/684-1140

Follett Software Company
1391 Corporate Drive
McHenry, Illinois 60050-7401
815/344-8700

Library of Congress
Cataloging Distribution Service
Customer Services Section
Washington, D.C. 20541-5017
202/707-6100

Library Systems and Services
The Library Resource
200 Orchard Ridge Drive
Gaithersburg, Maryland 20878
301/975-9800

Library Technologies Inc.
1142 E. Bradfield Road
Abington, Pennsylvania 19001
215/576-6983

MARCHIVE, Inc.
P.O. Box 47508
San Antonio, Texas 78265
210/646-6161

Sirsi Corporation
689 Discovery Drive.
Huntsville, Alabama 35806
205/922-9825

WLN
P.O. Box 3888
Lacey, Washington 98503-0888
206/923-4000

Providers of Bar Code Labels

Appendix C

Bar Code Discount Warehouse
14761 Water Ridge Parkway
Strongville, Ohio 44136
216/273-4746

Barcode Systems, Inc.
15315 Minnetonka
Industrial Road
Minneapolis, Minnesota 55345
612/945-9333

Blackwell North America, Inc.
6024 SW Jean Road, Building G
Lake Oswego, Oregon 97035
503/684-1140

Creative Data Products
P.O. Box 5637
Greenville, South Carolina 29606-5637
803/848-1070

Data Composition, Inc.
1099 Essex
Richmond, California 94801-2185
510/232-6200

Data Recall, Inc.
2175 Martin Avenue
Santa Clara, California 95050
408/980-5200

Graphic Technology, Inc.
301 Gardener Drive
Industrial Airport, Kansas 66031
913/764-5550

Image Scan
865 Waterman Avenue
East Providence, Rhode Island 02914
401/751-6505

Library Systems and Services
The Library Resource
200 Orchard Ridge Drive
Gaithersburg, Maryland 20878
301/975-9800

Library Technologies Inc.
1142 E. Bradfield Road
Abington, Pennsylvania 19001
215/576-6983

MARCHIVE, Inc.
P. O. Box 47508
San Antonio, Texas 78265
210/646-6161

Timeline for Automation Implementation

Appendix D

(Completion dates are included as an example of one library's experience.)

By Whom	Target Start Date	Completed Date	Action Needed
Staff	18 Oct. 1994	18 Oct. 1994	Begin implementation of board decision.
LH	18 Oct. 1994	18 Oct. 1994	Order book carts
JS	18 Oct. 1994	18 Oct. 1994	Organize implementation teams.
JS/LH	18 Oct. 1994	20 Oct. 1994	Order the data conversion processing from Auto-Graphics.
Staff	18 Oct. 1994	21 Oct. 1994	Order dumb bar codes for the books.
JS/LH	18 Oct. 1994	20 Oct. 1994	Order the hardware to begin the data conversion process
JS/LH	18 Oct. 1994	20 Oct. 1994	Order automation software and bar code readers.
Staff	18 Oct. 1994	15 Dec. 1994	Announce automation project to public.
Staff	21 Oct. 1994	21 Oct. 1994	Bar code report from Bar Code and Borrower Card team.
Staff Team	4 Nov. 1994	1 Nov. 1994	Report of Data Conversion Team on set-up of art gallery.
Staff Team	8 Nov. 1994	8 Nov. 1994	Retun profile for data conversion to Auto-Graphics.
JS	9 Nov. 1994	9 Nov. 1994	Schedule telephone move with service company.
Staff Team	9 Nov. 1994	18 Nov. 1994	Report of Public Awareness and Instruction Team.

By Whom	Target Start Date	Completed Date	Action Needed
Staff	11 Nov. 1994	8 Nov. 1994	Recommend chairs for data conversion room.
JS	11 Nov. 1994	8 Nov. 1994	Order chairs for data conversion room.
Staff Team	18 Nov. 1994	8 Dec. 1994	Preliminary report from Patron Registration Team.
Staff Team	23 Nov. 1994	March 1996	Preliminary report of Computer Deployment Team.
Telephone Service	23 Nov. 1994	10 Nov. 1994	Move telephone from TS office to data conversion room.
Bar Code Vendor	30 Nov. 1994	28 Nov. 1994	Bar code labels delivered.
Staff	Dec. 1994	Began 2 Nov. 1994	Close the library's art gallery for six to eight months while completing the data conversion project.
CSC	1 Dec. 1994	11 Nov. 1994	Set up computers in art gallery for data conversion project.
Staff Team	9 Dec. 1994	5 Dec. 1994	Report from Borrower Card Team. Design sent to GTI for preliminary mastering.
Staff Team	9 Dec. 1994	9 Dec. 1994	Preliminary report of Job Description Team.
CSC	16 Dec. 1994	16 Dec. 1994	Load the automation software.
Staff	19 Dec. 1994	15 Mar. 1995	Load the data.
Staff Team	21 Dec. 1994	16 Mar. 1995	Begin data conversion project.
Staff	6 Jan. 1995	20 Jan. 1995	Preliminary report from Circulation Policy Team.
CSC	25 Jan. 1995	30 Jan. 1995	Complete cabling.
JS/LH	1 Mar. 1995	27 Feb. 1995	Order remaining software.
Staff Team	Jun. 1996	July 1996	Complete data conversion.
Staff	May–Jun 1996	Jun. 1996	Register borrowers. Give them new cards and add patron records to system.
Board	Jun. 1996	Jun. 1996	Revise circulation/fine policy to reflect automation system.
Staff/Board	Jul. 1996	Aug. 1996	Open system to the public and begin checking out books.

Glossary

10 BASE-T CABLING: An implementation of the Ethernet Standard over unshielded twisted pair wiring (which is similar to wiring used for the modern phone system).

ATTIC GLEANINGS: Used books that people give the library. Some titles are in better condition than identical titles on the library's shelves. The standard catalogs help identify recommended titles a librarian may have missed.

AUTHORITY CONTROL: Establishment of one accepted "authoritative" form of a name or subject.

AUTOMATION MODULES: Major programs or functions of an automated library system. For example, an automated system may consist of a circulation module, an online module and a cataloging module. They are called integrated if they are connected through the software and work together.

BAR CODE READERS, CCD: (Charged Coupled Device), used to optically identify or read an item or patron bar code

BAR CODE READERS, LIGHT PENS: A device resembling a pen with a penlight on the tip used to optically identify or read an item or patron bar code. Connected to the computer between the key board and the CPU (Central Processing Unit).

BAR CODE READERS, NON-PROPRIETARY: Universal bar code readers that can read any standard bar code. Bar code readers that have not been modified to read only a certain automation system's bar codes.

BAR CODE READERS, PROPRIETARY: Bar code readers that have been modified with a chip that enables it to read only the symbology of a particular automation system.

BAR CODES: An array of parallel rectangular bars and spaces that together represent a single data element or character in a particular symbology. The two most popular bar codes in libraries are Code 39 and CODABAR.

BAR CODES, BI-DIRECTIONAL: Bar codes that can be read from either direction. This is important when you want to check-in or check-out large batches of books or when you do the inventory.

BAR CODES, DUMB: Bar code labels that do not have a bibliographic record linked to them when they are purchased. Data records are linked to them in the data conversion process.

BAR CODES, ORPHANED: Smart bar code labels for which the library has no books. They are created when the books they would normally be attached to are lost or stolen from the collection without the loss being noted on the shelflist card.

BAR CODES, SMART: Bar code labels that have been created from the library's bibliographic records and have been linked to a specific bibliographic record in the library. They have the title of the book and the call number printed on them.

BOOLEAN SEARCHING: A powerful searching that uses the terms "and," "or," and "not" to narrow or broaden a search.

BRAINSTORMING: Technique used by groups to generate ideas to reach a common goal.

CD-ROM: Compact Disk-Read Only Memory. A very high density storage medium used for audio or print data. It is often used for library catalogs and as a source for MARC cataloging records.

CD-ROM BIBLIOGRAPHIC UTILITY: A compilation of MARC records created by an organization or corporation that has a large database of bibliographic records. These records are loaded on a CD-ROM and marketed to libraries for a variety of purposes including data conversion.

CENTRAL PROCESSING UNIT (CPU): The main component of a computer. It is the main component of a microcomputer. It functions as the brain of the computer, executing and managing all the computer functions. The CPU is usually housed in a case by itself, separate from the monitor and the keyboard, and in a microcomputer it contains a single, extremely powerful microprocessor.

CHART OF GIVING: A scale often used in fundraising campaigns that divides the target amount into segments.

CLIENT-SERVER: An increasingly popular trend in data and information management where the software used to interact with the user (client) is separate from the software that actually manages data (server). The user (client) relies on the server for data and software computing power.

CONCENTRATOR: A device used to join communications channels from several different network nodes or segments.

DATA CONVERSION: The process of putting bibliographic records, the contents of the card catalog, on the computer and linking those records to a bar code that is attached to the book.

DOS or MS-DOS: Disk Operating System developed by the Microsoft Corporation for use on IBM or IBM-compatible personal computers (micro computers). It is the program used by the computer to control the access and transmission of data to and from the disk and the computer.

ETHERNET: Popular protocol and cabling scheme that controls the electronic traffic in a network with a transfer rate of 10 or 100 megabits/second.

EXPORT: Transferring data from the library's database to another database is referred to as exporting data.

FILE SERVER: A powerful microcomputer that usually has more computing power, specialized software, and more storage capacity than other computers. Because it is the host for all of the automation software and the data files, and because of the way it is configured, it cannot be used as a workstation.

GIGABYTE: One billion bytes. Often used to express the capacity of disk storage. Newer microcomputers used for business are often equipped with one gigabyte hard drives.

GRAPHICAL USER INTERFACE: An interface delivered by the microcomputer's operating system that allows the user to select files, programs or commands by using a pointing device such as a mouse to select pictorial representations on the screen.

IMPORT: Transferring records from another source to a computer database is referred to as importing data.

INTERNET: A telecommunication network linking hundreds of thousands of local and regional computer networks around the world. The Internet is used by students, scholars, researchers and reference librarians to access information that is in electronic format.

JACKS, KEYED RJ-45: Special type of connector that looks like a standard telephone connector. One end fits into a receptacle in the computer's network card or wall plate. Keyed jacks have a special channel in the receptacle and a key that fits the channel on the other half of the connector. This keeps the computer network from being confused with a telephone line connection.

JARGON: The special language of people in a particular business or profession. Doctors and nurses use medical terms or abbreviations, similar to spoken shorthand, to communicate with each other.

MARC: MAchine Readable Cataloging is cataloging that conforms to the national standard for communicating and storing cataloging data in a computerized format. The MARC format is used by the Library of Congress and by most automated library systems and bibliographic utilities.

MEGABYTE: One million bytes. The term is often used to express the capacity of memory or disk storage. A microcomputer may come with 8 MB of RAM (random access memory) and a 840 MB hard disk.

MODEM: Modulator-Demodulator. A device that enables changing a digital signal from a computer to an analog signal and then back to a digital signal again. Enables two or more computers to communicate with each other over conventional telephone lines via dial access.

NETWORK CARD: A computer device that is installed in the computer to enable it to be part of a network. It has a plug-in that looks like a telephone jack. Cabling, similar to telephone cable is run from the network card in the computer to the building's network wiring. Each computer on the network needs a network card.

NOVELL NETWARE: Networking software of choice for larger networks. Pricing is based on the number of users on the network.

NUMERIC IDENTIFIERS: Specific numbers that have been attached to each edition of a title that is unique to that edition. These numeric identifiers include the ISBN (International Standard Book Number) or the LCCN (Library of Congress Card Number). You can usually find these numbers on the copyright page of the book. Each format or edition (paperback, hardback, or book club edition) will have a unique ISBN.

ONLINE PUBLIC ACCESS CATALOG (OPAC): This is the library's computerized card catalog. It consists of all the library's bibliographic records and the software to search those records. Your library automation software will determine what your OPAC looks like and how easy it is for your patrons to use.

RAM: Random Access Memory. It is the computer's internal memory chips used to temporarily store data that can be read or written to while the computer is operational. RAM is volatile and any data in RAM are erased when the power to the computer is turned off or fails. RAM is measured in kilobytes or megabytes, e.g., 640K, 16 MB. RAM is sold and installed by SIMM, which means Single Inline Memory Module.

SOFTWARE RELEASE OR UPGRADE: Enhancements to the software made by the software company to make the software work better or perform new functions. It is like a new edition of a reference book.

STAND-ALONE SYSTEM: A single computer used for automation. It is not connected to another computer. All library functions (cataloging, searching and circulation) are performed on the same computer.

SYMBOLOGY: Term used to describe the way bar code labels are designed and read. Some products carry more than one so that they may be read by a variety of systems. Different UPCs use different symbology.

TOPOLOGY: Physical configuration of a network. It defines the hardware and the means used to connect the pieces together.

UNIX: A multi-user and multi-tasking operating system originally develop by AT&T. It has become increasingly popular because it is structured in a fashion that makes it easier to operate on many different types of computers on the same network. Unix is the operating system of choice when designing open systems. Unix is most often used in mini-computers as opposed to micro-computers which use MS-DOS or Windows.

UPC: Universal Product Code; the bar code symbol that is the standard in the retail marketplace.

UTP: Untwisted Pairs of cable for computer networks.

WINDOWS is an operating system also developed by the Microsoft Corporation. It allows the use of graphics, which are more user-friendly, rather than the character commands used by DOS. Windows operates in cooperation with DOS. It acts to extend DOS capabilities.

WINDOWS 95: Operating system from the Microsoft Corporation. Its graphical user interface makes it easier for users to access files and work with them. Included with this operating system is good, though limited, networking software. DOS is no longer needed with the installation of Windows 95.

Index